THE
Victorian Express

Dot & Alex,

Enjoy your ride!

Kristin Holmes   David Watson

THE Victorian Express

Text and Photography by

Kristin Holmes & David Watersun

Beautiful America Publishing Company

The Carson Mansion, which appears on the front cover and the preceding page, is perhaps America's most famous Victorian. Designed by Samuel and Joseph Newsome, the Carson Mansion was commissioned in 1884 by lumber baron William Carson. More than one hundred craftsmen from Carson's mill in Eureka, California, were kept employed during a local depression to work on the mansion, which took two years to complete. Carson featured the various woods he sold at the mill in the intricate, handcarved detailing throughout the structure. The Queen Anne exterior features an eclectic combination of architectural elements including: gables, balconies, porches, moldings, pillars, bargeboards, brackets, and finials. Carson's mansion epitomizes the imagination, skill, and extravagance that characterized architecture of the Victorian Era.

Published by
Beautiful America Publishing Company©
P.O. Box 646
Wilsonville, Oregon 97070

Design: Michael Brugman
Linotronic output: LeFont Typography

THE VICTORIAN EXPRESS

Library of Congress Cataloging-in-Publication Data
Holmes, Kristin, 1955-
The Victorian Express / text and photography by
Kristin Holmes and David Watersun.
p. cm.
Includes bibliographical references and index.
ISBN 0-89802-568-0 : $39.95. — ISBN 0-89802-565-6 (pbk.) : $29.95
1. Architecture, Victorian—United States. 2. Architecture,
Modern—19th century—United States. 3. Architecture—United States.
4. Architecture—United States. I. Watersun, David, 1952- . II. Title.
NA710.5.V5H64 1991
728' .37'097309034—dc20 91-18503
CIP

Printed in Hong Kong

Producing this book
personally enriched our lives,
brought us closer together,
and fulfilled a lifelong dream.

The Victorian Express
is dedicated to our parents,
whose support, guidance, and spirit
helped to make this book possible.

TABLE OF CONTENTS

The Victorian Experience *An Invitation to the Gilded Age* 1
The Victorian Era *A Timeline from 1837-1901* 3
The Victorian Express *A Historical Introduction* 7
The Victorian Essence *An Explanation of Styles*............................13

Towns with a Legacy

Cape May, New Jersey 37
Savannah, Georgia 57
Eureka Springs, Arkansas...77
Galveston, Texas...95
Marshall, Michigan...115
Galena, Illinois 133
Dubuque, Iowa 151
St. Louis, Missouri..169
Topeka, Kansas...189
Georgetown and Aspen, Colorado 207
San Francisco, California..229

Directory of Street Addresses 257
Architectural Glossary 262
Bibliography...269
Acknowledgments 273
Index..277

THE VICTORIAN EXPERIENCE
An Invitation to the Gilded Age

The Victorian experience offers a richly rewarding realm of American history, culture, and architecture. During the Victorian Era, which encompassed unprecedented political, economic, and social changes, the United States sought a cultural identity to express its growth, individuality, and imagination. Victorian architecture manifested this process as American architects and builders expressed their values in the diversified structures they created.

While the original owners of these eclectic Victorians are now silent, they leave us with a conspicuous collection of inimitable design statements from the past. The effort and expense required to create these unique buildings were extravagant, as the wealthy Victorian aristocracy indulgently built palatial homes to celebrate their elite lifestyles. Many of these magnificent mansions have survived the test of time to offer valuable examples of traditional American architecture in the 1800s.

An examination of Victorian architecture raises many questions. Why did American architects incorporate such divergent styles? How did the rapid westward expansion of America during the 1800s affect its architecture? What influence did technology such as the transcontinental railroad system have upon Victorian homes in the United States?

The Victorian Express, a pictorial survey that examines over a hundred of America's exemplary Victorians, invites the reader to appreciate the quality of these monuments. A dozen towns, from coast to coast, are featured which epitomize Victorian communities. Their history, culture, and architecture are depicted in words and images that reveal the essence of each region. The styles, personalities, and events that contributed to the evolution of the Victorian Era are discussed throughout the book, to provide insight into the atmosphere of the nineteenth-century.

The Victorian Express involved three years of research, travel, and production. Co-authors Kristin Holmes and David Watersun traveled over thirty thousand miles through forty states to study and photograph the Victorians portrayed in this volume. This publication is not intended to document these buildings so much as it is meant to celebrate the originality, ingenuity, and diversity of American Victorian architecture.

Researching and photographing these Victorians was a complicated logistical challenge. Current owners helped to supply historical background information about their homes, which the authors compared to archival material provided by local historical societies, museums, and libraries. Before they were selected for inclusion in the book, potential residences were evaluated for aesthetic appeal, in terms of color, authenticity, and current condition. Many of the houses were surrounded by visual obstacles. Therefore, whenever possible, architectural eyesores and distracting, extraneous items, such as power lines, telephone poles, and road signs, were cropped from the photographs to enhance their appearance.

This collection represents a visual interpretation of America's best Victorians and a historical discussion of the forces that created them. After studying these structural survivors of the Victorian Era, the reader will gain a new perspective of the role that traditional Victorian architecture has played in America. Hopefully, this exposure to the Victorian experience will inspire concerned individuals to help in the preservation of these unique landmarks. In that spirit, the authors invite historical enthusiasts, residential renovators, and lovers of Victoriana to enjoy their personal journey on *The Victorian Express.*

THE VICTORIAN ERA

A Timeline of Events from 1837 to 1901

1837
Queen Victoria begins her sixty-four year reign known as The Victorian Era.

1838
Louis Daguerre records photographic images with the daguerreotype process.

1839
"Balloon Framing" industrializes the residential construction industry.

1840
American railroad construction surpasses canals in mileage and cost.

1841
Fort Laramie is garrisoned as a major stopping place on the immigrant trail.

1842
The popular *Cottage Residences*, by Andrew Jackson Downing, is published.

1843
Expansionists call for the annexation of Texas and the acquisition of Oregon as the Great Migration to Oregon begins.

1844
Samuel Morse sends the telegraph message, "What hath God wrought" from Washington, D.C., to Baltimore.

1845
U.S. Congressman Robert Winthrop declares: "It is our manifest destiny to spread over this whole continent," as the U.S. Congress adopts a joint resolution for the annexation of Texas.

1846
California and New Mexico are annexed by the United States, as Brigham Young leads Mormons to the Great Salt Lake.

1847
Failure of the revolution in Germany forces the exodus of endangered German political refugees to the United States.

1848
Gold is discovered at Sutter's Mill near Sacramento, precipitating the frenzied California Gold Rush across America.

1849
The Pacific Railroad Company begins rail service west of the Mississippi River between St. Louis and Kansas City.

1850
The Compromise of 1850 calls for a declaration that Congress has no right to interfere with state slave trading.

1851
Over fifty thousand emigrants move westward by way of the Oregon Trial, as California officially becomes a state.

1852
U.S. Congress orders a survey across America for transcontinental railroad.

1853
The Crystal Palace Exhibition in New York City debuts Victorian designs.

1854
The Kansas-Nebraska Act by Congress permits state governments to control slavery, causing riots and bloodshed .

1855
John Roebling completes a wire cable bridge at Niagara that revolutionizes American bridge building techniques.

1856
Henry Bessemer perfects the method for converting pig iron into steel for industrial and railroad development.

1857
The U.S. Supreme Court rules in the Dred Scott decision that a slave is not entitled to the legal rights of a citizen.

1858

Gold discovery near Pike's Peak, Colorado launches an invasion of prospectors in the Rockies.

1859

The first major silver strike in the United States, the Comstock Lode, is discovered in the foothills of Nevada.

1860

First Pony Express relay rider leaves St. Joseph, Missouri for Sacramento, California.

1861

The Civil War erupts on April 12 with the Confederate attack upon Fort Sumter in Charleston, South Carolina where by eleven states secede to join the Confederacy.

1862

The Homestead Act enables settlers to acquire public domain lands, creating fifteen thousand new Western farms.

1863

President Abraham Lincoln issues the Emancipation Proclamation, offering freedom to slaves in the United States.

1864

Ulysses S. Grant is named Commander-In-Chief of Union Forces; General Sherman marches his army "to the sea" across Georgia and captures Savannah.

1865

The Civil War ends, and President Lincoln is assassinated by John Wilkes Booth, a crazed secessionist who blames Lincoln for the fall of the South.

1866

The Internal Revenue Service collects over three-hundred-million dollars in taxes to defray the costs of repairing damages from the Civil War.

1867

The United States astutely buys Alaska from Russia for only seven million dollars.

1868

The Fourteenth Amendment to the U.S. Constitution is ratified, giving civil rights to blacks under Federal Law.

1869

The first transcontinental railroad is linked on May 10 at Promontory Point, Utah. The rail lines, built by mostly Chinese and Irish laborers, are joined by a symbolic gold spike.

1870

A financial panic follows "Black Friday," when Jay Gould and James Fisk conspire to purchase all gold in the money market and sell it for profit.

1871

Mark Twain coins the phrase "The Gilded Age" to describe the later part of the Victorian Era.

1872

More than a half-million immigrants arrive at ports of entry in the U.S.A.

1873

The cable streetcar is invented by Andrew S. Hallidie to transport riders over the hills of San Francisco.

1874

St. Louis' Eads Bridge is built across the Mississippi River for westward passage from the "Gateway City."

1875

Gold is discovered in the Black Hills of South Dakota.

1876

Alexander Bell patents the telephone.

1877

Rail transportation halts when railroad workers on Eastern and Midwestern rail lines strike to protest wage cuts.

1878

America's first electric incandescent light bulb is made by Thomas Edison.

1879

Map research is completed to produce the first U.S. Geological Survey.

1880

Galvanized fencing and barbed wire are used to fence off tracts of the Western frontier for open range cattle grazing.

1881
Sitting Bull surrenders and advises Indians to lay down their rifles, claiming that it is futile to continue fighting against the white man, who had ravaged the buffalo herds.

1882
Over a quarter-of-a-million Germans emigrate to the American Midwest to escape European economic depression.

1883
The U.S. Civil Service begins operation.

1884
Charles A. Parsons patents the steam turbine for electrical power plants.

1885
Beef prices crash after cattle ranges are overstocked during the cattle boom.

1886
The people of France give the United States the Statue of Liberty, with an inscribed message on its pedestal: "Give me your tired, your poor, your huddled masses yearning to breathe free."

1887
Queen Victoria celebrates her Golden Jubilee after fifty years of monarchy.

1888
George Eastman perfects the handheld camera, introduced as the "Kodak."

1889
Last of the buffalo herds are wiped out by the insatiable demands of white men; meanwhile the first steel frame skyscraper is built.

1890
The "frontier" is officially closed according to the U.S. Census Bureau.

1891
Over five million women work in American factories and businesses.

1892
Rudolf Diesel invents his oil engine, as gasoline-powered tractors are tested.

1893
A financial panic is unleashed as the U. S. gold reserve falls below its "safe" minimum of one hundred million dollars.

1894
A severe drought across the Midwest causes complete crop failure, and half the settlers of western Kansas and Nebraska abandon their family farms.

1895
Guglielmo Marconi, helped by Thomas Edison, invents the wireless telegraph.

1896
Henry Ford first builds his highly popular "Model-T" automobile.

1897
Boston builds America's first urban subway train system.

1898
The United States wins the Spanish-American War. After victory at Manila Bay, America is given Puerto Rico and Guam; U.S. Congress buys Philippines for twenty-million dollars.

1899
Germany, Russia, Britain, France, Italy, and Japan accept the United States "Open Door" policy for China, assuring commercial access for all traders in the Chinese market.

1900
The railroad network expands to one-hundred-ninety-three thousand miles across the United States.

1901
Queen Victoria dies, and is succeeded to the throne by her son, King Edward VII.

THE VICTORIAN EXPRESS

A Historical Introduction

During the Victorian Era, Americans rode along the fast track of history, steaming along as a nation fueled by ambition, pulled by destiny, and steered by leaders who promised light at the end of each tunnel. The passengers are gone, but many of the places they called home remain alive with the history and architecture of their lives. As we share their heritage with you through words and photographs, we invite you to experience a vicarious adventure across Victorian America — we call this literary journey *The Victorian Express*.

What is *The Victorian Express*? It is the retrospective examination of a diverse and fascinating period in American history. What many architectural historians call "The Victorian Era" in the United States borrows its label from a British monarch, and it is chronologically measured by the reign of Queen Victoria who ruled Great Britain without interruption from 1837 until 1901. During this era American voters elected seventeen different presidents to the White House, and the United States changed in character as often as its chief executives. A vast whirlwind of political, economic, social, and religious forces inspired unbridled American growth.

No country in the world grew more quickly or substantially than the United States during the 1800s. At the political heart of this expansion was a doctrine called Manifest Destiny, which led many Americans to believe that it was their sovereign right and national purpose to acquire and develop new territories for their country. Prominent New York newspaper editor John L. O' Sullivan wrote in 1845, "It is the fulfillment of our manifest destiny to overspread the continent allotted by Providence for the free development of our yearly multiplying millions."

The United States dramatically increased its population from six million in 1800 to seventy-six million by 1900. National political leaders were eager to acquire more territory for their burgeoning electorate. As pioneers pushed westward and southward through North America to claim new lands and resources, their actions were politically sanctioned by the Federal government. Those that resisted — the Indians, Mexicans, Canadians, and the last defenders of the French and Spanish empires — were economically and militarily coerced to abandon their previous strongholds.

Beginning with the Louisiana Purchase in 1803 and culminating with the Spanish-American War in 1898, the expansionist policies and actions of the United States tripled its size from one million to almost three million square miles. This growth secured its incomparable acquisition of wealth and power as the United States became the most ambitious country of the nineteenth-century.

As American expansion reached the Pacific Ocean important transportation and communication links were made between the Eastern establishment and the Western frontier. Canals and railroads were built with the help of inexpensive immigrant labor at a phenomenal pace. Riverboats steamed up and down the Mississippi River, carrying passengers and freight to St. Louis, the gateway to the West. By the end of the nineteenth-century, over one hundred fifty thousand miles of railroad lines and waterways provided diverse transportation routes for interstate commerce.

The railroads carried public news and private correspondence between Eastern metropolitan centers and Western developments. Midwestern railroads published enticing accounts that extolled financial opportunity and domestic security for frontier settlers. For example, from a brochure for the Chicago, Kansas & Nebraska Railway: "An invitation is hereby extended to everybody desiring a choice home in the finest country in the world. Come to northern Kansas and locate in the state that is always at the front. Bring your family to the state that offers you fertile lands, prosperous towns, plenty of churches and schools, and no saloons."

As gold, silver, and other valuable minerals were discovered in the Sierras and Rockies, countless claimstakers swarmed the mountains and extracted unprecedented wealth from mining strikes. Flourishing trade and access to new markets boosted the economy of many hub cities that were strategically located on railroad lines and waterways. Hunters brought elegant furs from the northern wilderness to river towns, where their bounties were exchanged for provisions and manufactured goods. Precious minerals were transported by train from the mountains to metropolitan jewelers for sale to affluent urban buyers.

Many families eagerly resettled along the frontier trails, hoping to realize their dreams for prosperity and personal freedom. Entire railroad towns were rapidly built in a few weeks along the major commercial routes in a frenzy of speculation and opportunism.

Settlers in remote areas, such as the Rocky Mountains, relied on the railroad's capability to deliver mail order catalogs and periodicals featuring the latest lifestyle trends, creature comforts, and construction plans for building their Victorian houses.

The prospect for trade, commerce, and profit in key Western frontier towns attracted entrepreneurs from the urban East, who brought with them an affection for architectural grandeur. During the boom times of the 1800s, many newly-made millionaires capriciously built luxurious mansions to glorify their financial status, often erecting Victorian castles in the wilderness as reflections of their wealth. Social life assumed a superficial quality, whereby a man's home was the measure of his character, and the Victorian monuments that the wealthy built for themselves displayed a shameless mix of conspicuous construction and unabashed opulence. Architectural fantasies competed for attention among the nouveau riche, and excessive exterior exhibition set the stage for unprecedented interior extravagance.

With the increase in mobility among wealthy nineteenth-century Americans came a desire to build playground resorts for the rich. In the eastern United States, it became fashionable for affluent urban families to visit summer residences along the Atlantic seaboard in places like Cape May, New Jersey. Simultaneously, residents of the Midwest visited resort communities in the Ozarks like Eureka Springs, Arkansas, whose mineral waters offered legendary power for curing physical maladies and providing rejuvenation. Following the gold rush in California, San Francisco became a hedonistic Mecca for mining millionaires, who threw their gold nuggets around town like spare change.

The extravagant lifestyle of the Victorian aristocracy plagued the American economy with roller coaster repercussions. Unrestrained land speculation, wildcat investment schemes, and unregulated banking practices precipitated catastrophic crashes, widespread unemployment, and economic depression. Although America surged ahead with the bravado of expansionism, it stumbled repeatedly during four major financial panics in 1837, 1857, 1873, and 1893, which crippled new residential construction.

Towns and cities rose and fell with the economy. With each wave of optimism came real estate speculation, and Victorian architecture thrived. Corruption and greed exploited each surge of progress as debt and poverty flooded the market with financial chaos. A cyclical economic pattern dominated the Victorian Era and left a schizophrenic mark upon its architecture.

To find strength and hope amidst the economic uncertainties of the times, Americans turned to their leaders for direction. Greed and corruption were blamed for many of America's economic woes, and social activists led dramatic crusades for civil rights. The issues of slavery were debated, and intensified conflict eventually led to the Civil War. The war caused massive personal loss and property destruction requiring extensive national reconstruction.

After the Civil War, the demand for housing intensified as millions of immigrants from Europe flocked to the United States, bringing with them strong social and religious traditions. These groups tended to settle collectively in certain areas of the country, which gave specific regions and communities a distinctive sense of their heritage. The Victorian architecture these immigrants adopted for their new homes often represented a symbolic connection between their transplanted lifestyle and geographic origins. In response to this popular demand for residential housing, nineteenth-century American architecture precariously progressed through dramatic incarnations in search of a style it could call its own.

The United States consequently became an awkward amalgamation of political expansion, economic unpredictability, and social diversity. These unsettling forces challenged the nation to seek a new identity during the second half of the nineteenth-century. America continued to explore its lifestyles and architecture in response to accelerated growth and unbridled power.

Victorian architecture became an expression of these exploratory times as a new breed of architects broke traditions to create styles that were both innovative and unforgettable. The architectural inspirations of Andrew Jackson Downing, François Mansart, Richard Norman Shaw, and Henry

Hobson Richardson all left distinctive signatures on the mercurial face of Victorian architecture in America.

At least seven major trends surfaced during the Victorian Era to compete for popularity among Victorian home builders. Industrialization and transportation made plans and resources available for American families to build, landscape, and furnish their homes. Popular Victorian pattern books that circulated around the country, such as *Hobb's Architecture* and *Sloan's Homestead Architecture*, offered hundreds of house designs, landscape drawings, and furniture suites to rural mail order customers.

The individual house builder freely adapted these generic blueprints to suit his particular situation. It is very unlikely to find two identical Victorians in the country today, since each building typically became a unique creation of the tastes, skills, and income of its owner. Victorian architecture became accessible to the general population, but it remained adaptable to the regional supply of building materials and the technological resources of its builders.

As a result, American folk architecture was born, combining local techniques and distant architectural influences to create personalized residences for its inhabitants. From coast to coast, various styles were invented, copied, and added to the repertoire of the home builder. This whimsical synthesis of elements gives Victorian architecture an individuality unparalleled in the history of the United States and offers insight into the inventive and playful nature of the American imagination throughout the 1800s.

Much of what epitomized American Victorian architecture has been lost to the forces of nature. Earthquakes in the West, floods in the East, hurricanes in the South, and tornadoes in the Midwest have all taken their toll on these vulnerable structures. Even more destructive have been the ravages of fires, since many Victorians were built primarily of wood. Erosion of time and neglect have ruined many other houses.

Until quite recently the wrecking ball of progress, in the guise of urban redevelopment, leveled many unique architectural treasures. Despite all of these threats to their longevity, many splendid Victorians survive today as testaments to their time. They stand rescued, renovated, and repainted for our appreciation, like grand old survivors against the odds.

What follows are some of the best examples of these survivors, located in quaint towns and bustling cities across America. This book contains current photographs of our favorite Victorians from Cape May to San Francisco, and it discusses how these unusual houses were built during an era of dreams and challenges. Throughout America there is a revival among Victorian enthusiasts, who have saved and resurrected this unique phase of American architecture for our enjoyment and as a gift to the future.

Many Victorian buildings are protected as National Historic Landmarks. In some cases, entire town districts have been preserved for posterity by the efforts of their proud citizenry as living examples of historical heritage. As you turn the pages and admire these vintage homes, let yourself experience their traditional elements of style and grace combined with the novelty of color and invention. They express the essence of American Victorian architecture. Lend us your imagination, and enjoy your personal ride on *The Victorian Express*!

THE VICTORIAN ESSENCE
An Explanation of Styles

The United States underwent a dramatic transformation during the Victorian Era, from a generally rural, agricultural economy to a diverse conglomeration of Eastern urban factories, Southern plantation ports, Midwestern gateway cities, and Western frontier towns. Until the 1830s, Americans lived essentially as they had since Colonial times, but by the end of the nineteenth-century their lifestyle had embraced the perks and pitfalls of progress. Transportation networks, communication links, and international trade propelled America to eminent status as a world power.

As American manufacturing evolved from handmade items in small workshops to mass production in large factories, merchandising also shifted from simple country stores to glamorous mercantile palaces. This transformation from an individualized economy of craftsmen and shopkeepers to a hierarchy of industrial and retail barons, employing millions of company workers, created two classes in America: the elite entrepreneurial millionaire and the typical wage earner. The invention of machines to serve the ruling class and dominate the working class divided Americans into the nouveau riche, and the common man, who dreamed of striking it rich.

The new rich erected edifices to their fortunes — palatial mansions that commanded admiration from their peers and envy from their workers. The managers who ran these manufacturing and retail empires achieved their own form of status; this new middle class of homeowners built less grandiose houses with elements that emulated the style of their affluent employers. Least wealthy and most prevalent were the tradesmen, laborers, and clerks, who owned or rented simple cottages that suited their ordinary lifestyle.

The Victorian home came to symbolize its owner's stature in life, and as such it was the most important material acquisition an aspiring person selected in the nineteenth-century. The scale and appearance of a home conspicuously displayed one's financial achievement, social status, and prestige in the community. Furthermore, the home was decorated to project the personality, taste, and character of its owner.

Commercial establishments and civic architecture also changed in form and function during this era. Rural taverns and country inns were replaced by ornate hotels in the growing cities across America. As municipalities grew from frontier towns, dignified public buildings, schools, and churches were constructed to serve the civic needs of Eastern immigrants accustomed to urban culture.

The challenging task of designing these private and public structures was shared by architects and master builders across America. As the Victorian Era began architects on the East Coast provided builders in the West with generic handbook plans that were often modified to suit the material resources, tools, and expertise of the local builder. When technology and building techniques improved Victorian designs became more complex and sophisticated, culminating with the elaborate styles popularized at the turn of the century.

A spectrum of styles emerged during the Victorian Era: Gothic, Italianate, Octagon, Second Empire, Queen Anne, Romanesque Revival, and Folk Victorian. The architects and builders of American Victorians were not imitators, rather structural innovators who experimented on their own terms. Americans never intended to copy the traditional motifs of Europe; they used them as sources of inspiration to develop a unique style, which made use of the new materials and tools available on the frontier. What evolved was a collection of distinctively American architecture that surprised and delighted its designers, builders, and owners. Today we share their pride and appreciation.

Gothic Revival
1840–1880

The term "Gothic" encompasses a variety of religious and secular architecture. Inspired by the medieval churches of Europe, the Gothic Revival movement began in England during the early 1800s and spread to America by 1840. In the nineteenth-century, "Modern Gothic" or "Rural Gothic" were terms used to describe this style.

Most architectural historians believe that the Gothic Revival movement was an attempt to escape the harsh realities of an industrial culture and return to the romance of the Middle Ages. Writers such as Sir Walter Scott wrote intriguing novels with brooding medieval settings that helped popularize the Gothic genre. Scott's vivid writing featured cruel barons, heroic knights, and fair damsels against a backdrop of castles, abbeys, and monasteries — imagery that inspired Gothic Revival architecture.

A.W. Pugin was an English architect as well as an adept etcher and pen-and-ink artist. As a leading exponent of the Gothic Revival movement, Pugin published several books on medieval architecture that included detailed illustrations of buttresses, pinnacles, crockets, and drip moldings. Architectural pattern books like these, along with romantic imagery in literature,

translated medieval elements into a nineteenth-century style suitable for designing Gothic rural and suburban residences.

Professional architects who were formally trained in Europe began to emigrate to the United States in the early 1800s. These men were not only schooled in classical architecture — they were also familiar with the Gothic Revival movement that was developing in England then. America offered them an arena for mixing traditional architecture with romantic innovations, such as the introduction of Gothic residential interpretations.

A popular supporter of the Gothic Revival movement was architect Andrew Jackson Downing, who thought that Gothic elements added a tranquil and picturesque quality to domestic designs. Downing contended that a comfortable home required spaces that matched their functions, and his philosophy encouraged architects to vary room sizes and shapes to fulfill their intended purposes. In its residential form, Gothic architecture was an innovative style, which liberated America's emerging middle class from the spatial constraints of tightly-clustered city row houses.

The prominent identifying features of the Gothic Revival style are: a steeply-

pitched roof with high cross gables, gables that have decorated vergeboards, and wall surfaces extending into gables without eaves or trim. Gothic windows commonly extend into gables, and their window frames frequently have pointed-arch shapes. Romantic Gothic Revival houses feature irregular combinations of elongated rooms, protruding porches, and bay windows to evoke a medieval quality.

Most Gothic Revival houses were constructed from 1840 to 1860 in the Northeast, where the architects lived that popularized this romantic style in America. They are less common in the South, where Greek Revival architecture dominated the residences of the region. Scattered examples, however, can still be found in most areas of the United States that were settled before the late 1800s.

Steeply pointed gables with decorated vergeboards are the most exemplary characteristics of a Gothic Revival design. The finials rising above these gables, and its traditional board-and-batten siding, distinguish this Gothic Revival building.

THE VICTORIAN ESSENCE, *An Explanation of Styles*

Italianate
1840–1885

While the Romantic School of architecture embraced the Gothic Revival movement as a progressive expression of the American domestic lifestyle, traditionalists extolled the classic virtues of Greek and Roman structures. When English scholars visited the Mediterranean during the first half of the nineteenth-century, they observed how buildings, such as Italian farm villas and Renaissance palaces, had often incorporated ancient motifs into contemporary designs. These researchers returned to England with detailed renderings of their studies, which inspired a movement among architects to infuse their blueprints with renewed classicism.

British versions of Italian-inspired buildings, called "Italianate" architecture, proliferated in England during the early nineteenth-century. The Italianate style refers to any house or commercial building that uses Italian shapes and details, including elements of the Renaissance Revival, Tuscan Villa, and Italian Villa patterns. Just as the Gothic Revival movement penetrated American culture with the immigration of English architects, advocates of the Italianate movement also journeyed to the United States and introduced classic forms to American residential and civic architecture.

The Italian Villa style surpassed the Gothic Revival movement in the United States as the romance of Italy captured America's imagination. The growing prosperity of the Victorian middle class allowed more Americans the luxury of visiting the cultural Meccas of Europe. When they returned to their home country, romantic rural Americans built their own version of Italian villas in the country, while nostalgic city dwellers constructed Renaissance Revival town houses.

Italian style houses in America were not necessarily custom-designed by architects. Many Italianates were constructed by builders who took familiar structures from generic pattern books and simply added Italianate details because they were fashionable. An inspired builder might add wide overhanging cornices, scrolled ornamental brackets, or a square cupola on the roof to embellish his Victorian with Italianate accents.

The Italianate style was versatile, and it adapted readily to almost any kind of construction or location. Since it was derived from classic elements, an Italianate could be quite simple and symmetrical, which made its graceful lines ideal for peaceful settings. The inspiration for Italianates, however, originally came from the vernacular buildings of rural Italy, where the hilltop villas were perched upon rugged landscapes, and the bold terrain demanded buildings with irregular, asymmetrical profiles.

The prominent identifying features of the Italianate style are: two or three stories, a low-pitched roof with widely overhanging eaves and decorative brackets, and tall, narrow windows. The window frames were frequently arched with elaborate inverted crowns; prominent windows had heavy, molded architraves. Many Italianates were topped with a square cupola or tower built at the apex of hipped roofs, which were covered with zigzag patterns or contrasting bands of colored slate.

The Italianate style dominated American houses that were constructed from 1850 to 1880. It was particularly popular in the expanding towns and cities of the Midwest, as well as in the many older, but still-growing cities along the Northeastern Seaboard. Italianate houses were least common in the Southern states, where the Civil War, Reconstruction, and financial depression in the late 1800s discouraged new home construction in the South until after the Italianate style had passed from fashion in America.

Italianate houses have several derivative styles; the most prevalent are the Italian Villa, portrayed here, and the Formal Renaissance Revival row houses, frequently seen in San Francisco. This classic Italian Villa design features numerous characteristic details, including a cupola, brackets, and hooded windows.

Octagon
1850–1870

Perhaps the most unusual architectural style to gain prominence during the Victorian Era was the Octagon. In 1641 one of the first American polygonal buildings, an octagonal wooden church, was built in the Hudson River Valley. The English Colonists built numerous gazebos in private gardens and public parks in America, but it wasn't until the nineteenth-century that octagonal buildings became conspicuous. Thomas Jefferson was an early supporter of geometric houses. Thirty of the fifty buildings that he designed as an avid amateur architect were either polygon-shaped or featured polygonal rooms.

The most dedicated proponent of the Octagon style was an eccentric innovator named Orson S. Fowler. Originally a theology student, Fowler discovered that he had a knack for phrenology, the peculiar Victorian pastime of analyzing a person's personality by feeling bumps on the head. Fowler turned what began as a simple parlor trick into a lucrative career, and he became a popular personality on the traveling lecture circuit. By mid-century, Fowler had syndicated a personal advice newspaper column; he also owned a successful publishing company through which he distributed several best-selling books that espoused his unique philosophy.

Fowler felt that "nature's forms are mostly spherical — to enclose the most material in the least compass," and he mathematically proved that an octagon contains one-fifth more area than a square with the same perimeter. Fowler's house designs included an encircling porch and central stairwell, thus providing easy access to all rooms without requiring dividing hallways, which could cause "unhealthy drafts." Fowler maintained that the Octagon style was superior because it "increased sunlight and ventilation" by eliminating "dark and useless corners," and its eight exposures provided twice as much sunlight as a square house exterior.

Fowler would have preferred basing his ideal houseplan on the circle, which he saw as the most natural and efficient way to enclose the greatest amount of interior space. Recognizing the limits of most builders' skills, however, he was willing to settle for a six-, eight-, or sixteen-sided structure. Fowler scoffed at "finified carvings and cornicing," and he argued for simplified building exteriors. He reasoned that more functional, less ornate designs, such as his Octagon style, would provide affordable, durable housing for the working class.

After Fowler first promoted his ideas on the lecture circuit in 1848, an Octagon style movement swept the nation for the next decade. During the 1850s hundreds of octagonal houses were built across the country according to his theories. Occasional examples were based on ten-, twelve-, sixteen-sided, and totally rounded forms. They sprang up in modest numbers across the United States, particularly in New York, New England, and the Midwest, with many small towns boasting just one Octagon. Many of Fowler's unique designs were also used for schools, barns, and churches.

Octagon houses are very rare today, since only a few thousand were originally built in the 1800s. This unique structure is probably the country's only octagonal Victorian with a dome. The detailed brackets, bull's-eye windows, and intricately carved columns are uniformly placed to complement its symmetry.

Second Empire
1855–1885

During the reign of Louis Napoleon, from 1852 to 1870, Paris was considered to be the cultural center of Europe. The grand avenues of the French capitol were lined by tall, ornate buildings with distinctive roofs that fulfilled the monarch's notion of architectural dignity. The style became known as "Second Empire" as it gained popularity throughout France.

Two international expositions, held in Paris during 1855 and 1867, exposed this Second Empire style to the rest of the civilized world. Drawings and engravings of Parisian buildings circulated throughout Europe where its style was immediately imitated. Architects in Germany, Italy, and England constructed similar buildings, but it was in America that the Second Empire style earned keen endorsement.

Americans visited France, like Italy, as part of the fashionable "Grand Tour of Europe." The beauty of Paris, with its picturesque boulevards and harmonious architecture, left a cultural impression on American visitors. Therefore, beginning in the early 1860s, examples of the French Second Empire style began to appear in American architectural designs.

Architects trained in France also emigrated to the United States during the nineteenth-century, and their arrival brought distinctively French influences to the American architectural arena. The majestic style of French urban architecture impressed American government leaders who commissioned Second Empire projects for federal, state, and city public buildings. Once civic leaders started the Second Empire trend in America, private builders soon followed suit; residential and commercial buildings topped with an unmistakably French roofline spread across America during the 1860s.

The "Mansard" roof, as it was coined, was not a new design when it was introduced to American Victorian architecture. It was first derived from Italian sources, and it had been used in Europe since the early 1500s. The man who popularized the stylish roof and gave it his name was François Mansart (1598–1666), who became noted for applying classical details to embellish contemporary buildings.

The principal feature of a Mansard style building was a roof that sloped down the top story at a forty-five degree (or more) pitch, with dormer windows built into its steep sides, and the upper remainder of the roof covered with a flat-pitched deck. Usually the Mansard roof was built with a convex curve, but variations featured concave or S-curved shapes. Molded cornices often bound the lower roof slopes, and decorative brackets were usually found beneath the eaves.

The Mansard roof became popular because it converted unusable attic space into a livable extra floor. Unlike a peaked roof, a Mansard roof allowed for efficient use of the attic, and its characteristic dormer windows let in an abundance of light. In France, homeowners were taxed by the number of floors in their houses. Since the top floor of a Mansarded house was technically the attic, the Mansard design gave French owners a tax break.

Second Empire buildings were normally designed with symmetrical elevations, and the main entrance was always the central feature of the front facade. This style was a dominant motif for American architecture constructed from 1860 to 1880, and was even endorsed by President Grant's chief architect. Unfortunately, scandalous politics of the era tainted its future and precipitated the style's demise. Second Empire was most popular in the Northeastern and Midwestern states; it was less common in the West, and relatively rare in the Southern states, although scattered examples survive in all regions of the United States settled before 1880.

The Second Empire style is easily recognized by its steeply sloped Mansard roof with dormer windows. Its window framing and cornices are similar to those found on Italianate houses. Distinctive roof silhouettes vary from straight, as shown here, to concave, convex or S-shaped curves. Mansard roofs are frequently decorated with contrasting patterns, colors, and textures of roofing material; the flat-pitched roofs are often topped with cast-iron cresting.

Queen Anne
1880–1910

By the 1870s many American architects had become dissatisfied with the romantic revivals of past European architectural styles such as Gothic Revival, Italianate, and Second Empire. As the United States developed its own political and cultural identity towards the end of the nineteenth-century these progressive architects agreed that their country needed a totally original style of architecture as well. American architects studied the great civilizations of the past and saw that each major empire had expressed its cultural values in a signature style of architecture. They wondered why the United States could not also develop an indigenous structural identity for its buildings that manifested the heart and mind of the American spirit.

A similar search for identity occurred in England during the same decade when British architects and builders realized that their previous revivals of European themes had failed to develop an original style of architecture in their homeland. They too had relied on revamped amalgamations of old styles rather than introducing innovative architectural ideas to their structures. American and British architects were equally stifled as they wrestled with their creative frustration and common need for a

revitalized approach to future designs.

Architectural pundits on both sides of the Atlantic mutually heralded Richard Norman Shaw, an English architect, as the forefather responsible for their liberation from revivals of romantic European styles. Shaw introduced an original type of architecture that was labelled "Queen Anne." This popular title was actually a misnomer, since "Queen Anne" houses did not closely resemble buildings of that Queen's reign (1702-1714). Moreover, Shaw's unique interpretation effectively assimilated and redefined the whole experience of the English Renaissance. By using half-timbering and a profusion of gables, Shaw created a new style that paid homage to England's medieval Tudor cottages without reviving or imitating them.

The Queen Anne style was first introduced to American architects at the Philadelphia Centennial Exposition of 1876 when British exhibitors premiered several of Shaw's model buildings. American architects perceived Shaw's style as a cultural link to their own heritage in the same way that British enthusiasts associated his novel designs with similar English characteristics. Architectural attitudes in both countries underwent a dramatic transformation

during this period of liberation: from a Medieval to a Renaissance perspective, from traditional to more progressive construction techniques, and from previously predictable to more sensational displays of building designs.

The introduction of Queen Anne architecture to the United States catalyzed American opinion. The Exposition served as the impetus for American architects who saw the Queen Anne style as an English example that could be inexorably transformed into an American vision. Architects in this country were convinced that the potential to invent a truly American style existed. By synthesizing Shaw's innovative ideas with their own imaginative designs, construction techniques, and building materials, American architects created a distinctive new hybrid breed of Queen Annes.

Conical towers, multiple gables, and contrasting shingle patterns were inventively combined to create elaborate, multifaceted Queen Anne architecture.

The Queen Anne style covered a broad range of variations and adaptations with the most prominent styles being Stick, Shingle, and Eastlake. Popular during the late 1800s, Stick architecture was a transitional genre, which associated the medieval qualities of the Gothic Revival movement with Queen Anne modifications. Wood was utilized more conspicuously by extending beyond its use in the internal framework to also serve as an external finishing material.

The builders of the Stick style broke with the parochial parameters of the past and incorporated more diverse influences from the building styles of Switzerland and Japan. They augmented the long and complex development of Renaissance design by opening the field to cross-cultural possibilities. In spite of its rather eclectic conglomeration of gables, balconies, towers, verandas, pendants, and diagonal braces, Stick was one of the less exuberant of the late-nineteenth century expressions.

Stick is classified by some architectural historians as a wooden, polychromatic version of the High Victorian Gothic. Although architectural pattern books displayed many designs in the Stick style, relatively few were constructed in comparison to the popular Italianate and Second Empire styles of the era. Architectural examples of the Stick style survive principally in the Northeastern United States where most were constructed during the 1870s.

Another derivative form of Queen Anne architecture was the Shingle style, built mostly from 1880-1900, which applied layers of shingles in uniform colors and textures to the exteriors of Queen Anne houses. Wooden shingles became the American complement to Shaw's "Old English" tile-hanging. The inventive use of these shingles by prominent architects such as McKim, White, Emerson, Price and Richardson, created a sensation in the United States.

As political scandals, social discord, and economic upheaval beleaguered most Northeastern cities in the late 1800s, many wealthy urbanites responded by escaping the stress of city life for sojourns to the seashore during weekends and the holidays. The result was a boom in resort housing development along the Northeast Coast, and the Shingle style reached its highest popularity along the Atlantic Seaboard. At fashionable seaside destinations such as Newport, Cape Cod, Long Island, and the Maine coast, affluent families often built summer houses in this Shingle style.

Shingle-style houses and cottages were functional as well as fashionable, since they were built to withstand the very hot summers and extremely cold winters of the Northeastern coastal region. Surviving Shingle structures are relatively uncommon today except in coastal New England. These American interpretations often employed complex patterns, shapes, and layers of sheathing, typically combined with large entrances, turrets, bays and wraparound porches. Precisely styled roof lines were produced by carefully trimming the overhanging shingle ends in curved profiles. Although scattered examples of Shingle designs were evident across America, inspired by the lavish publicity of architectural magazines at the peak of its popularity, Shingle architecture never gained national acceptance like other derivations of the Queen Anne style, such as Eastlake.

Eastlake architecture, sometimes also referred to as Spindlework, prevailed from the 1870s to the 1890s in the United States, and it describes a certain mode of decoration on Queen Anne houses. Charles Eastlake, an English architect, published his book *Hints on Household Taste* in 1868, which generated an enthusiastic response in America. Eastlake was not one of England's most prominent architects, nor did his book create much excitement in England. Nevertheless, his ideas had a tremendous influence on architects and builders in the United States, and his popular book sold out in six editions by 1881.

In his writing Eastlake eloquently argued for a return to integrity in construction, sound craftsmanship, and harmonious architecture. He emphasized the need for architectural fundamentals by reasoning that designs should be adapted to their materials, and functions should be expressed, not

A variation of the Queen Anne design was the Stick style with its steeply pitched roof and ornamental gable trusses. Squared towers, clapboarded sides, and decorative layers of stickwork distinguish Stick style homes which were built from Connecticut to California.

concealed. He objected to deceptive and superficial ornamentation such as painted imitations of marble patterns, veneered woodwork, and ostentatious wallpapers.

The principles that Eastlake reiterated were clearly articulated, but his endorsement of craftsmanship was exaggerated through the overt indulgence of his zealous followers. American proponents of Eastlake enthusiastically embellished their houses with a plethora of stylized posts, turned knobs, geometric wood cut designs, intricately carved panels, spindle-and-spool balusters, and complicated lattice work — all profusely displayed in conspicuous excess. Wood served as the ideal raw material for this carefree construction because it was readily available throughout the country, and it lent itself easily to erecting economical balloon frame construction.

The salient elements of the Queen Anne style included: steeply-pitched roofs of irregular shapes, usually with dominant, front-facing gables, patterned shingles, cutaway bay windows, and other devices used to avoid a smooth-walled appearance. Queen Anne facades were decidedly asymmetrical with partial or full-width porches that were usually one story high and extended along one or both side walls. The diversified and multifaceted dynamics of Queen Anne architecture gave it a less predictable look than the more symmetrical styles that preceded it in the Victorian Era.

The Queen Anne style, which culminated with the fanciful Eastlake interpretations of the 1890s, dominated American residential architecture through the end of the nineteenth-century. Its overt influence was less prevalent in the more traditional Northeastern states where most homeowners chose to exercise greater decorative restraint. By contrast, the most extroverted examples of Queen Annes were generally built in the West and the New South. In these territories unbridled color and form celebrated the wild frontier spirit, and outlandish entrepreneurs often built extravagant Victorians that matched their egos, imaginations, and bank accounts.

Ultimately, the prolific and excessive use of ornamentation in Eastlake architecture precipitated a retreat from Victorian styles by American architects at the end of the nineteenth-century. After decades of unorthodox exploration with Queen Anne derivations, many architectural purists returned to their original goal of seeking a more essential American style. Neo-Colonial styles resurfaced, and the United States completed the most dynamic cycle of experimentation in its architectural history. During this ebullient era of self-discovery and exuberant expression, American architects and builders stretched the limits of their imagination and gave this country a unique identity.

The "Gingerbread Mansion," a Victorian landmark in Northern California, is an excellent representation of the Queen Anne Eastlake style with its many lathe-turned spindles and detailed woodwork.

THE VICTORIAN ESSENCE, *An Explanation of Styles*

Romanesque Revival
1880–1900

The Romanesque Revival style , like the earlier Gothic Revival movement, had its origins in medieval Europe, particularly in the churches of England, France, and Germany. Romanesque buildings featured heavy masonry with rounded arches and thick, fortress-like walls. The first American usage of the Romanesque style appeared during the 1850s in public buildings like the Smithsonian's interpretation of the Renwick Castle.

Decades passed until Henry Hobson Richardson (1838-1886), an American architect trained in Europe, revived Romanesque architecture in a profoundly personal style that became known as "Richardson Revival." Richardson arrived on the American scene when eclecticism was at its peak. Although his early training in France was in the Classic and Renaissance styles, he turned to the Romantic School for inspiration in his designs.

Richardson, who was influenced by the work of Richard Norman Shaw, incorporated elements such as half-timbering into his urban architecture. Richardson initially introduced the monumental style only in public buildings and churches, but later he translated its proportion and scale to Victorian city residences. Richardson's

Romanesque adaptations became very popular for large public buildings during the 1880s, but he completed only a few more houses in this style.

Richardson was not the only American architect to explore the Romanesque tradition for ideas, but his thorough research revealed the inherent qualities and spirit of the style. With his personal insight and vision Richardson continued to perfect these forms, motifs, and details in each of his successive buildings. Richardson could simplify his plans and identify each project's most important elements; he possessed the unique talent to express both strength and beauty through his designs, which were equally powerful and graceful.

With its respectable qualities Romanesque Revival architecture came to represent the solid foundation and civic prosperity of American urban culture in the late nineteenth-century. At the peak of his architectural career Richardson met an untimely death in 1886; a flattering monograph on his life and work was published, which further increased public interest in his style. Builders continued to use his popular designs during an 1890s' resurrection that established public and private buildings across America in the Richardson Revival style.

Largely through Richardson's influence, the Romanesque Revival style became associated with: masonry walls, usually with rough-faced and squared stonework, asymmetrical facades with round towers and conical roofs, and round-topped arches over windows. Because they were always of solid masonry construction (stone veneering techniques were not yet perfected), Richardsonian Romanesque structures were much more expensive to build than other Victorian styles which could also be executed in wood. For this basic reason Richardson's monumental buildings are primarily architect-designed landmarks, located in the larger cities of the Northeastern United States, but scattered examples of his work also exist in a variety of metropolitan areas across America.

Towers, masonry walls with rough-faced stone-work, and rounded arches over windows and porches are the identifying features of the Romanesque Revival style. The overall shapes of these buildings are often similar to Queen Anne houses; however, the massive quality of their impressive signature stonework creates a more formidable appearance.

Folk Victorian
1870–1910

As the American economy transformed into an industrial and mercantile hierarchy during the Victorian Era an urban working class emerged, comprised of factory laborers, retail clerks, and company employees. This group needed affordable and appealing housing while it struggled to climb the ladder of free enterprise. In more rural areas American settlers relied on their own ingenuity and resources to build houses that were functional and which also expressed a style reflective of their original hometowns. American Folk Victorian architecture, despite its simplicity, reflected the pride of these homeowners.

"Folk Victorian" architecture (1870-1910) could best be described as a vernacular style that is identified by the presence of Victorian decorative detailing on simple folk house forms. Most of these structures were built by local carpenters who borrowed ideas from Victorian pattern books and ordered supplies of pre-cut detailing from local trade centers. The growth of the national railroad system made it possible for pioneers on the frontier to acquire prefabricated components from distant wood mills across the country. The railroads also brought woodworking machinery to settlers in remote regions where craftsmen at the building site produced similar detailing from local materials.

Most Folk Victorians had some Queen Anne spindlework detailing, but these houses were easily differentiated from true Queen Annes, because their symmetrical facades, homogeneous textures, and unvarying wall surfaces betrayed their authenticity. Other detailing was borrowed from Italianate designs; the most popular locations for embellishment were the porch and cornice line. The porch supports were commonly modeled to resemble either Queen Anne-type turned spindles or square posts with the corners beveled.

Although Folk Victorian houses varied slightly in each region of the country, its architecture generally included the following elements in some improvised combination: porches with spindlework detailing or flat, jigsaw-cut trim, symmetrical facades with gables, and cornice-like brackets. Other elements of the Folk style varied throughout America. Front-gabled homes were most common in the Northeastern states, and one-story, narrow, shotgun forms were generally found in the urban South. Side-gabled one- and two-storied buildings were built throughout the West, while pyramidal structures with Victorian detailing were constructed almost exclusively in the Southern states. Easterners designed small, understated cottages, built in deference to the conservative styles that prevailed in the more established neighborhoods.

Folk Victorian, or Vernacular style, was the typical architecture of the working class. Its relatively simple style was created by carpenters, who borrowed building ideas from generic pattern books. Railroads transported precut detailing, derived from Queen Anne and Italianate motifs to remote settlements, where porches and cornices were decorated with embellishments sent from distant mills.

THE VICTORIAN ESSENCE, *An Explanation of Styles*

Preceding the Victorian Era, color played an insignificant role in American architecture. Colonial homes were built before paint was readily available, and Greek Revival houses in America were whitewashed to resemble the ancient white marble temples that inspired them. Churches, courthouses, and town halls were painted white throughout the United States to add respectability.

During the first half of the nineteenth-century wooden Victorian buildings received the obligatory white coat of paint, with shutters painted green or black for contrast. With the emergence of Romanticism in American architecture, however, white was disdained by such influential architects as Andrew Davis and Andrew Jackson Downing who changed the urban landscape with their designs for Gothic Revival, Italianate and Second Empire houses. Their dynamic designs were a bold departure from the box-like appearance of the Greek Revival style, and they insisted that exterior colors added another dimension to their ornate detailing.

Downing repeatedly stated his aversion to white exterior paint; he suggested instead the use of natural, earthy "gray or fawn" colors for decorating Victorians. In his book *Cottage Residences*, published in the 1850s, Downing provided six tinted specimens on hand-colored plates to guide his readers towards the proper selection of exterior colors for their homes. Downing suggested that it was best to avoid colors not found in nature, since the paint palette should resemble the colors of the elements used to build the house: rocks, earth, wood, and so forth.

Residential architecture in America became more complicated in design during the last quarter of the nineteenth-century, and exterior paint colors also evolved into a more diverse spectrum. Progressive architects in the 1870s and '80s, such as Henry Hudson Holly, promoted a movement towards richer polychromatic schemes to decorate the intricate exteriors of the later Victorian houses. Queen Anne, Stick, Shingle, and Eastlake designs were deftly painted in rich color combinations ranging from deep earth tones of brown, terra cotta, and sage, to more vibrant shades of red and green.

The imaginative addition of architectural embellishments to these late-nineteenth-century Victorians challenged their owners to apply complicated color combinations which required meticulous planning and execution to succeed. Wood ornaments, gables, finials, porches, and decorative trims required the use of balanced paint hues to accentuate these elements. The relative size, shape, and position of each component within the Victorian facade were compared to determine the best plan for enhancing its qualities.

There were also regional and climatic influences to consider when selecting the ideal Victorian color treatment. The sunny Southwestern and Coastal resort areas of the United States tended to paint their houses with lighter, brighter colors, often using more vibrant shades to animate their architecture. More traditional regions, such as the South and New England, continued to show a bias towards white and neutral tones in deference to the conservative precedents established by the Greek Revival and Colonial styles.

More recently, the "painted ladies" colorist movement which started in San Francisco during the 1960s has spread across the country to popularize a new spectrum of "boutique" colors. Today's Victorian homeowners often paint their homes as a neo-traditional form of self-expression. Sensitivity, taste, and good judgment are essential prerequisites for determining whether to use "historically correct" or "boutique" colors. Only time will tell what colors tomorrow's Victorians will be painted.

It is not unusual to find polychromatic paint schemes that use over twenty different colors on a single house. The position, size, and shape of each element within the exterior facade must be considered to determine the ideal palette for painting a Victorian house.

Stained glass windows, radiant and ever-changing screens of colored light which transform interior space, have fascinated man for over a thousand years. Usually associated with the great cathedrals of the Middle Ages, the stained glass window became an American art form with the revival of medieval styles of architecture in the nineteenth-century. Thousands of these windows were made for churches, public buildings, and private residences across the United States.

The name that has become synonymous with stained glass is Louis Comfort Tiffany; son of the legendary jeweler Charles Tiffany. As a child, Louis was dazzled by the array of glittering jewels in his father's store. This early inspiration certainly seems to have been reflected in his lifelong love and devotion to the world of glass. When Tiffany began his experiments in glass, he set out to discover what secrets the medieval masters knew that enabled them to produce such sparkling masterpieces.

Tiffany took up the medieval style of coloring molten glass with metals and chemicals, such as iron oxide for green, gold or selenium for red, and cobalt oxide for blue. To these centuries-old techniques he added original tricks to produce iridescence, opalescence, and undulating textures. Tiffany's expertise with glass reflected his unbounded love of the material. He poured and rippled it with custom devices, gathered and folded it with pincers and gloves into drapery glass, and finally sprinkled it with glass flakes and studded it with jewels. His palette ranged from delicate pastels to nacreous midnight tones with startling blotches of vivid hue.

About 1890, just when John La Farge and Louis Tiffany were gaining a reputation for their "opalescent art glass" windows, the style of Art Nouveau emerged from France and Belgium. The ecclesiastical market had always been Tiffany's bread-and-butter, but he was no longer content to produce just windows. He aimed his sights at a new market — decorative objects for the American home. Tiffany was determined to use the artist's medium as a message to the masses, hoping to help people distinguish the beautiful from the banal. His glasshouse began turning out blown-glass vases and bowls trademarked "Favrile," meaning handmade. Tiffany aptly translated the spirit of the Art Nouveau movement in America. The creations displayed in his Corona, New York studio earned him national and world acclaim.

By 1900, the Corona operation stored over five thousand different colors and textures of glass. With waste from window production running into the tons by 1899, Tiffany launched a new line of stained glass electric lamps to use up the scraps. Success of the Tiffany lamps was insured by the availability of Edison's incandescent bulbs. At the peak of Tiffany Studios, these extremely popular lamps were produced by the thousands each week. Tiffany's dream, however, to bring art to the masses was not feasible, since the cost of his lamps often exceeded the annual salary of many American wage earners.

Today's experts see Tiffany's art glass of the period as a microcosm of modern art history. The flower of American stained glass emerged about 1860, burst into twenty years of glorious bloom from 1880 to the turn of the century, and then saw itself slowly wither away by the 1920s. Today, a few small studios have recaptured this art, creating originals as well as producing authentic replicas of Tiffany's windows, lamps, and vases.

Stained glass designs interpreted in contemporary and traditional styles are created by a handful of skilled artisans across America. The authentic reproduction of original Tiffany lamp designs has become a specialized craft, as manifested by this Wisteria lamp, which was recreated from a nineteenth-century Tiffany pattern.

An early map, dated 1744, shows a "flash light" at Cape May Point; however, the first known lighthouse was not built until 1823. Unfortunately, the original lighthouse was undermined by the tides in 1847, and a second one, built one-third mile from the present site, was also lost to the sea. The current lighthouse, built in 1859, is one hundred seventy feet high, with eight-foot-thick walls at the base. The original beacon, consisting of several oil lamps focused by six hundred fifty-six prisms and lenses, remained its source of light power until 1938.

CAPE MAY

Queen of the Seaside Resorts

*Right: **At the peak of its popularity in the mid-1800s, Cape May's promenade was lined with colorful multi-tiered oceanfront resorts. Every room had its own view of the beach, and most seaside hotels offered porches and balconies for the comfort of their guests. The Sea Mist typifies the popular use of awnings that prevailed in Cape May.***

Our journey upon *The Victorian Express* begins on the Atlantic seaboard where a Dutch captain named Cornelius Jacobsen Mey explored a sandy peninsula in the Delaware Bay area in 1620, the same year that the ship Mayflower first carried the Pilgrims to the New World. Captain Mey surveyed the finger of land, noted the mild climate and potential for settlement, and bestowed his name on the point as "Cape Mey," what has become called Cape May, New Jersey.

Many of the area's earliest European settlers were only two generations removed from the tiny band of hardy Pilgrims who landed at Plymouth Rock. Genealogical surveys have retraced the Cape's bloodlines and proclaim it "A Lost Colony of Mayflower Descendants." Pirates secretly cruised these waters in the 1600s, finding the Cape a perfect place to bury their treasures, acquire provisions, and effect ship repairs.

Left: **This Second Empire home with its Queen Anne tower, like many Cape May residences, was completely rebuilt after the Great Fire of 1878. There were at least three major fires before the town's worst blaze in the 1870s, which marked the end of a glorious era for elaborate wooden structures in the coastal resort town.**

Right: **Creative craftsmanship, imaginative detailing, and patient painting create entrances that epitomize Victorian homes.**

Whalers from New England sailed around Cape May in search of the sixty-foot leviathans that commanded thousands of dollars for their whalebones and blubber oil.

As overzealous whaling became less profitable at the end of the 1700s Cape May remained a sparsely populated area. Local residents turned to agriculture, ocean fishing, and shipwreck salvage for their livelihoods. To the north cedar swamps provided raw materials for a cedar shake industry but the limited supply of trees was quickly exhausted.

By the early nineteenth-century Cape May had developed a reputation as a seaside destination for fishing, crabbing, and swimming, or "bathing" as it was called. Philadelphia newspapers extolled the virtues of Cape Island, and several hotels, cottages, churches of various denominations, and a public school were constructed during the 1820s and '30s to serve resident and visitors. Housing sites increased in the 1840s as the first speculative real estate residential subdivisions sprouted up.

The unpainted buildings of Cape May were introduced to advertising by the owners of the New Atlantic Hotel, who broke with tradition by whitewashing the building and identifying their venue with story-high letters above the entrance. By 1850 twenty hotels competed for tourist business, and Cape May had gained moderate popularity for its pleasant atmosphere. Smooth, broad beaches of fine-grained sand sloped gradually down to the Atlantic surf, and because the town was at the end of the South Jersey peninsula it was cooled by both Atlantic Ocean and Delaware Bay breezes.

In the spring of 1852 work began on a new hotel that marked the transition of Cape May from a provincial New Jersey locale to a nationally known meeting place and site for one of the great resorts of the Western world. This new establishment, named the Mount Vernon in honor of George Washington's private retreat, was proposed to be the largest hotel in the world. The symmetrically shaped spa resort with its carefully proportioned pavilions and handsomely scaled porches, was to have almost one thousand guest rooms with first-class amenities.

After two years of construction the first wing of the great building was finished, and it was opened for the summer season of 1854. It was an extraordinary event that attracted the attention of the world's rich and famous. In the following year, royalty, millionaires, and celebrities came to the Mount Vernon to bask in the political, economic, and social limelight. Cape May's first newspaper was founded to cover the hotel's illustrious events and report the activities of the town's famous visiting personalities.

By 1855, Cape May had reached its zenith as a world class attraction hosting luxurious resorts with gambling halls for wealthy visitors. Prestigious families from Baltimore, Philadelphia, and Washington, D.C. enjoyed pleasant and efficient steamboat cruises across to the South Jersey peninsula, where they met for gala events at the Mount Vernon. But in September 1856 the new hotel was tragically burned to the ground in an uncontrollable fire that left its owners financially devastated, since they had failed to purchase fire insurance and the investors lacked the capital required to rebuild.

Cape May's misfortune became Atlantic City's opportunity. A new railroad linking Camden to Atlantic City isolated Cape May out on the peninsula, and the town sank into depression. For five years after the big fire, Cape May resembled little more than a ghost town, as the Financial Panic of 1857 and the dreary prospect of Civil War shifted the nation's attention and resources away from traditional resort retreats.

During the Civil War, the town population was generally divided in support between the North and the South, although the newspaper officially endorsed the Union cause. Of greater concern was the town's pressing need to compete with Atlantic City and its lucrative railroad route. In 1862, despite the ongoing war campaigns, Cape May lobbied for the construction of a railroad line down the Jersey peninsula.

This estate, built in 1879, was the home of Emlen Physick, a rather eccentric country gentleman who had to complete medical school to inherit the family fortune. He was never known to have practiced medicine, but he had a reputation for being different. He reportedly purchased undergarments for his chickens after they had been "defeathered" by the neighborhood's overzealous dogs.

Many of the Victorians in Cape May were moved from their original locations in town to more prestigious locations as their owners became more successful; a hundred years later, many of these vintage homes were moved again by preservationists. This home was sold in the 1960s for one dollar and the cost of moving the home to its current location. Originally built in 1880 for Cape May's City Treasurer, it was subsequently occupied by his daughters and hundreds of cats. The women painted the house pink, a unique color for Cape May then, and it has been known as The Pink House ever since.

Following the Civil War a new wave of financial speculation arrived in Cape May, led by prominent Philadelphia lawyer and developer John Bullitt. After acquiring the Columbia House, one of the largest hotels in Cape May, Bullitt and his partner hired a renowned Philadelphia architect named Stephen D. Button. Button designed various improvements for Columbia House and created a beach pavilion on the front lawn. The rich ornamentation and carefully detailed facade Button produced for the hotel marked a turning point in Cape May's architecture, since it was the first structure built by an important architect in more than ten years. Soon, other developers followed Bullitt's example, and many old hotels and summer houses were quickly resurrected along the South Jersey seashore.

By the arrival of the 1869 summer season Cape May was again a popular retreat for the victorious Northeastern urbanites. In less than a decade most of the old hotels had been rebuilt, along with civic improvements such as municipal water service and gaslight illumination for all major streets.

The most important project was the construction of a boardwalk and public access road along the beachfront, which created a handsome promenade and attracted the attention of outside investors. Vast tracts of residential lots were sold, and new Victorian summer houses were constructed

RESORT LIFE

Summer travelers seeking rest and relaxation flocked to the seashore to escape the hectic city life. Victorian vacationers went to these summer resort towns ostensibly "for the purposes of good health," since the ocean water and air were believed to rejuvenate both the mind and body. More likely, however, it was the opportunity to advance in social status by mingling with the affluent upper class that attracted many visitors to "take in the air" at seaside towns like Cape May.

For the social elite, lavish events were staged to introduce each other's families. Debutantes were announced to potential suitors, socialites entertained aristocrats at premier parties, and millionaires treated politicians to seaside junkets. These exclusive activities took place in Cape May's many summer cottages and hotels, where the "fresh air parlor" provided a discreet venue for intimate twilight conversations. These verandas were furnished with wicker rockers, which invited conversationalists to sit, relax, and confess their hearts and minds. Wicker "summer furniture" with its clean, cool, and comfortable quality, encouraged the rituals of courtship and gossip. Guests could unwind from their formality, reflect on the privacy of the moment, and perhaps share a secret or offer some friendly advice with their confidant.

Other resort town activities included bathing or napping in the morning, afternoon tea dances, and gala balls in the evenings. Another important pasttime for women was to stroll along the "Ladies Mile" on the boardwalk between the main avenue and the beach to admire each others fashionable attire. These elegant dress designs were commissioned from couturiers in Philadelphia and New York, and it was not uncommon for a well-heeled lady to change her outfit seven times a day.

For all visitors, rich and otherwise, the Cape May experience was epitomized by "bathing" at the seashore. Mixed bathing was not permitted, although modesty for women was not a problem, since their conservative bathing costumes covered most of the body. Once the white flag was raised, the ladies were taken out into the water in horse drawn bathing transports until the water was waist-deep. There they could emerge to wade in the water without exposing their legs. Once the red flag was up, however, only men were allowed at the seashore, so they could brazenly swim in the nude.

Despite sanctioned male nudity on the beach, resort life for women in Cape May was coyly Victorian. Occasionally, a fashion faux pas would upset the local gossip columnist who once wrote, "Brevity may be the soul of wit, but it isn't the proper mode for a Cape May bathing suit. The waist was cut low in the neck, showing shoulders of dazzling whiteness. Sleeves on the dress — there were none! Hardly the thing for Cape May."

Stephen Decatur Button, who had successfully established himself as a prominent architect in Philadelphia during the 1850s, arrived in Cape May in 1863 at the height of his career. Button came at the personal request of developer John Bullitt, who commissioned him to improve the appearance of Bullitt's recent hotel acquisition, Columbia House. Button's skillful application of detailed ornamentation to the Columbia's facade and the construction of a new beach pavilion on the hotel lawn initiated a new trend in Cape May architecture that had seen little innovation in years.

When rail service along the Jersey peninsula was extended to Cape May later that year, the demand for Button's architectural services increased dramatically. Over the next three decades, he designed over forty of the resort town's buildings in his signature style. Throughout his prolific career, Button created variations on bracketed Italianate designs that were widely imitated by local contractors and builders.

Urban architects in cities such as Philadelphia and New York gradually divorced themselves from these simple rectangular structures embellished with their thinly overlaid ornamentation. The residents of Cape May continued to embrace Button's more provincial cottage styles, which seemed to suit the casual resort atmosphere. During the late 1800s Cape May's detachment from the shift towards industrialization in Northern metropolitan centers sustained a traditional lifestyle that both preserved the town's distinctive seaside appearance and protected its architecture from the external influences of urbanization.

Although Button enjoyed what amounted to an architectural monopoly in Cape May, his personal impact on the town's development was not arbitrarily imposed. The unanimous respect that he commanded from his clients was earned through developing a classical attitude toward architecture. A biography written in 1892, when Button was eighty, remarked on his continuing preference for simple proportions and symmetrical designs, which distinguished his work from the frivolity and complexity of other contemporary Victorian architecture. It was clear that Button's designs had remained faithful to the style that he had cultivated over fifty years earlier during his formal training.

Through Button's prolific architectural contributions to Cape May, his work became intrinsically linked to the town's classic Victorian appearance. As a result, Button shaped Cape May's architecture for almost four decades during the years when the town's identity was established. Even after his death in 1897, Button's architectural firm continued to sell adaptations of his early models for another decade, and many of his buildings remain well-preserved today.

by many of Philadelphia's most important citizens. Despite a fire that burned several central blocks of hotels and shops in late August, the 1869 season was the most profitable in the town's history, and recovery was almost immediate.

The Cape May renaissance flourished until the summer of 1873, when financier Jay Cooke's bank unexpectedly closed. This event caused a national business panic, which rapidly escalated into a depression. Seashore houses and summer vacations became expensive luxuries, and most developments came to a standstill. The business depression of the mid-seventies ended most speculative development, and construction in town was limited to replacing losses from fire and storm. The railroad boom was over, but its impact had been enormous. Great hotels bordered the entire promenade, and new houses had completely filled the areas between the beach and the old town center.

Just as Cape May began to emerge from years of financial depression in 1878, the town was ravaged again by a terrible fire that burned beyond control for days. Despite heroic efforts by trainloads of special firefighters from Philadelphia, the fire could only be extinguished after the town center was totally incinerated; most of the summer cottages constructed during the previous residential boom were destroyed as well. Without the impetus of its railroad economy Cape May suffered chronic financial paralysis.

The town did not collapse after 1878, but Cape May developers were slow to take advantage of the opportunities for recovery. Instead of creating modern hotels to attract a new generation of cottage builders, the town's investors cautiously reconstructed similar structures on a smaller scale in the same style and on the same sites. This uninspired type of building attracted little new investment for the town, which prolonged a trend of slower recovery and less drastic urban renewal.

Despite the conservative economic climate during the 1800s, a grandiose effort was made by a group of local businessmen to develop the site of the old Mount Vernon

The Abbey, so nicknamed because of its church-like appearance, was designed by S.D. Button and built in 1870 as a summer residence for John B. McCreary, a wealthy Pennsylvania coal baron. McCreary made his wealth through an exclusive leasing arrangement with the railroads that assured priority for his own coal shipments, while allowing him to charge his competitors to use his freight service as well. The tower, trimmed with elaborate ironwork, stands over sixty feet high. This building is one of the few edifices in Cape May selected by the Historic American Buildings Survey as possessing such architectural significance that measured drawings of it are recorded in the Library of Congress.

Left: *Many of Cape May's architectural treasures, such as this iron fence, can be best appreciated by walking or bicycling through the town's tree-lined streets.*

Right: *The original owner of this house was a Delaware river pilot for over forty years; he built his home in 1882 at the cost of four thousand dollars. The current owners purchased the building in 1980 and have spent many times its original construction cost to restore The Queen Victoria to its present grandeur.*

Hotel to the west of town, which had remained barren ever since its 1856 fire. In 1884 they proposed an immense hotel for the site and constructed an office building in the shape of an elephant. The developers borrowed the idea of designing their structure in the form of a giant pachyderm from a bizarre elephant attraction recently built in Margate, New Jersey. Called the "Light of Asia," the elephant building was intended to attract new land development to the outskirts of town. With no local public transit, Cape May's commercial limits were restricted by the proximity of hotels and cottages to the railroad.

The failure of this scheme ended the last speculative venture in the resort community for a generation. By 1890, Cape May was overdeveloped with a fixed and aging clientele, and it no longer attracted real estate investors. The local community became increasingly introverted, scarcely trying to attract new summer business. Cape May made no effort to fight legislation that ended gambling, which had been a major attraction for visitors. The town residents' most outrageous act was to vote the town "dry" during an 1890 election. Overnight, saloons closed up and hotel bars became valueless. To the tippling summer tourists, it was a shock to arrive in alcohol-free Cape May.

By deterring the development of new monolithic resort hotels, these local conservatives effectively preserved Cape May's

Left: **This antique bird house, made by a Pennsylvania craftsman, is over one hundred years old and has been carefully painted by its current owners to match the colors of their home.**

Right: **This house was built in 1868 by Stratton Ware for his brother-in-law, Joseph Hall, and has had only three owners since the Civil War. The current residents boldly returned their home to its original colors much to the chagrin of the conservative neighborhood. Eventually, their colorful treatment inspired others in town to liven up their monochromatic paint jobs and transcend the traditional combination of white houses with green shutters.**

intimate scale and relative informality, which was exceptional for a late-nineteenth-century resort community. It was this prohibitive lifestyle that limited its future for the next generation. With the last of its traditional beach hotels completed by 1895, Cape May looked essentially as it would for the next half-century. Stephen Button's bracketed Italianate designs had been faithfully repeated in minor variations during four decades, and there was little prospect for change.

As Cape May entered the twentieth-century its role as a resort was very precarious. Compared to the newer developments in Wildwood and Atlantic City, most of its hotels were outdated in content and style. Construction had stagnated for more than a quarter of a century, while modern resorts had established new standards on a different and grander scale. The wooden hotels of Cape May appeared weathered and archaic in contrast to the substantial buildings of brick, steel and reinforced concrete, gigantic amusement piers, and great public buildings erected by the competition.

With the arrival of the automobile, daily trips to the Jersey shore became more popular than overnight stays. Cape May was a farther drive from metropolitan areas than other resorts, and its relative antiquity and isolation discouraged day visitors. The grand lifestyle represented by the great hotels had become passé. Cape May lost its reputation as a resort town and began to attract mostly permanent residents — retirees, fishermen, and military families from local bases.

Life in Cape May continued uneventfully until March 1962 when the sun and moon aligned to create exceptionally high tides. As the tide level reached its peak, an off-shore storm generated enormous waves that crashed across the Cape's beaches and brought disastrous flooding to the resort. Almost the entire town was submerged under flows of saltwater and sand, and the traditional wooden boardwalk was destroyed along the entire promenade.

Again Cape May was on the brink of ruin; without relief it would have sunk into oblivion. Federal disaster relief was forthcoming, but the government would not endorse or support a reconstruction plan that emphasized rapid and intensive commercial development similar to Atlantic City. Instead, the U.S. Department of Housing and Urban Development urged local officials to adopt a reconstruction plan that preserved the town's Victorian heritage.

A master plan was developed by imaginative architects and government officials to preserve and protect Cape May from future environmental and economic catastrophe. Government funding financed the construction of storm walls to protect the town against future flood damage. New roads, public buildings, and civic improvements made redevelopment attractive. Investors were offered tax incentives to modernize traditional hotels under the watchful guidance of historical preservationists, and new commercial projects such as restaurants and retail shops were subject to strict zoning.

Because of its successful Victorian town renewal project, Cape May in the 1970s emerged as a restored and revitalized community. In recognition of the preservation efforts by the city of Cape May and the local Mid-Atlantic Center for the Arts, Cape May was officially designated as a National Historic Landmark in 1976. The entire town was also listed on the National Register of Historic Places, a distinction

The Angel of the Sea, built in 1850, has just undergone an extensive, tasteful renovation. The original owner, William Weightman, was the son of the chemist who discovered quinine, and this house was financed with the commercial success of that discovery. When Weightman purchased an expansive ocean view property in 1881, the townspeople expected him to build another prestigious home. Instead, his existing home was lifted onto logs and moved to its second location. The home was placed at an angle to maximize the view of the Atlantic Ocean — a peculiarly modern idea in 1881. In 1963, the building was moved again to its present location near the sea.

CAPE MAY, *Queen of the Seaside Resorts*

Left: **A number of similar cottages on this block were built in 1872 by a local entrepreneur. These houses share common architectural elements in their vergeboards, paired-cornice brackets, and central third-story gables.**

Right: **Wood was the principal building material used in Cape May. Beyond it's structural utility, wood was also used as ornamentation for porch spandrels and roof acroterion, or as decoration on walls, over doors, and around windows. Lumber was turned, carved, and scroll-sawed into vergeboards to give interest to the eaves. Decorative wooden features were further enhanced by the application of colorful paint combinations.**

that has only been given to five communities in the entire United States.

Today Cape May thrives again as a place for visitors to escape from urban pressures and experience the tranquillity of its traditional Victorian atmosphere. Many of the renovated summer cottages operate as inns, boutiques, and antique shops. The larger hotels feature vintage restaurants, traditional music, and special evenings with Victorian themes. Historical walking tours, canopied bicycle trolleys, and authentic horse-drawn carriages fill the narrow streets with activity. Workshops, seminars, and festivals attract thousands of participants to town. Cape May; has survived fires, floods, and failures to reign proudly as "Queen of the Seaside Resorts."

Left: **This house, built in 1873, boasts the only convex Mansard roof in Cape May. It was the summer home for George McCreary, whose father, John, lived next door in The Abbey. George McCreary was a banker and philanthropist; his wife was one of Cape May's most prominent social figures who earned a reputation for being a fashion plate. The home remained in the McCreary estate until after World War II.**

Right: **This stained glass window in The Linda Lee combines many jewel-tone colors within its faceted glass, which emulates the Renaissance style first made popular in France.**

The Savannah Cotton Exchange, designed in 1886, was the first Savannah commission for architect W.G. Preston, a disciple of Henry Hobson Richardson. The front entrance faces the heart of the city, while the long balcony on the backside overlooks the historic cobblestone section of River Street along the Savannah River.

SAVANNAH

Southern Survivor

Savannah, Georgia has always depended on its strategic port location for survival. In 1733, James Oglethorpe and a group of English settlers founded the original town on a wide, moon-shaped bend in the Savannah River. Oglethorpe had persuaded King George II to establish a colony at this river location as a haven for poor and persecuted English expatriates, who in turn would provide new access for navigation and trade in the Colonial South.

The new port allowed deep-water ships to approach the south side of the Savannah River, where they could safely draw over twelve feet of water without grounding and easily transfer cargo across the forty-foot-high bluffs along the river. British traders realized the importance of building a commercial stronghold in Savannah. England sought to protect their Carolina colonies to the north by providing a buffer against their Spanish arch rivals in Florida.

The English Crown commissioned Oglethorpe to design plans for a city that could continue to grow as Savannah developed. Oglethorpe proposed a municipal grid system based on "wards," with public and private buildings placed in symmetrical patterns. Each of these urban sections included an open space surrounded by four residential plots to the North and South and four civic sites to the East and West.

Residences were built on larger land divisions, and community structures were erected on smaller complementary lots. A town square was at the center of this configuration, which gave each ward a central meeting place and provided paths between the buildings. Oglethorpe designated the nearby highlands beyond the original wards as "the commons," and the city planner reserved these areas to the east, west, and south for future city expansion. Oglethorpe personally supervised the development of the first six wards in the 1730s, and his original master plan was faithfully implemented years after his return to England in 1743.

In early Savannah, the colonists relied on community wells for fresh water which was pumped from the center of each town square. Domesticated animals such as cows, goats, and hogs were allowed to roam freely through the streets, and they quenched their thirst at the puddles that usually formed around these watering holes.

The Spanish presence in Florida impeded the progress of Savannah, because British interests were reluctant to invest in a port that was vulnerable to a hostile takeover. When the Spanish fleet retreated from the region in 1763, Savannah's significance as a maritime trade center increased. Rice, lumber, and cotton were barged down the Savannah River and loaded into British cargo ships, which returned with their raw materials to England.

When the American Revolution began in 1775, Georgia was the youngest, most remote, and most sparsely settled of the thirteen colonies. In spite of strong Tory sentiment, the spirit of independence prevailed, and the Royal Governor, James Wright, fled Savannah. The patriots held Georgia until December 1778 when the British came by sea and recaptured Savannah. American forces, aided by the French Navy, were repelled in 1779 when they tried to retake the city. The British were finally driven from Georgia in 1782 by local patriots and the Continental Army.

Several decisive setbacks plagued Savannah in the following years. Augusta was selected as the state capital in 1786, which diminished the political significance of Savannah. The majority of the port city's classical Colonial buildings were devastated by an uncontrollable fire in January of 1820. In the aftermath of the catastrophe, a disastrous yellow-fever epidemic killed seven hundred citizens in just five months and forced the evacuation of six thousand people, which equaled nearly eighty percent of the town population.

City, state, and private organizations rallied together to combat the dreaded disease. The Georgia Medical Society proposed elimination of the wet rice culture in the lowlands near the city, which effectively mitigated the epidemic during the 1820s and '30s. A city waterworks program replaced the town's open wells and cisterns with a piped, fresh-water supply system, thus eradicating many of the probable sources of the yellow-fever epidemic.

With its public health under control, Savannah's location began to attract renewed investment as a center for trade, transportation, and development. Several financial institutions, such as the Second Bank of the United States, opened

Ornamental ironwork is Savannah's most conspicuous common denominator. Ironwork was introduced by English architects in the late eighteenth-century as a carryover from their designs in England. Many foundries were established in Savannah, providing both simple and intricate lace-like patterns that were used extensively on local fences, railings, and balconies.

SAVANNAH, *Southern Survivor*   59

ELI WHITNEY

The agrarian South depended heavily on the growth of cotton to support its economy during the eighteenth- and nineteenth-centuries. As the northeastern United States became more industrialized in contrast to the Southern states, plantation owners found it difficult to profitably operate with their labor-intensive methods of cotton growing. Thanks to the ingenuity of an inventor named Eli Whitney the South was provided with the cotton gin, a machine that modernized cotton harvesting. Whitney's laborsaving device boosted plantation profits and revitalized the Southern economy.

As a farm boy in Massachusetts, Eli Whitney's only interest was to explore his father's shop, which was equipped with a variety of mechanical devices. Eli was preoccupied with manufacturing, and he persuaded his father to let him continue in mechanical work. Eli made and repaired violins, worked in iron, and at the age of fifteen manufactured nails during the Revolutionary War. When the demand for nails declined after the war, Whitney turned to making hatpins and almost monopolized the business in his state. While a student at Yale, he earned extra money by repairing problematic machines on campus.

After graduation Eli visited an associate's family plantation in Savannah. One evening a group of cotton growers were discussing a frustrating agricultural problem. Green seed cotton was an unprofitable crop, because separating cotton from its seed by hand was so tedious that it took a worker one entire day to obtain a pound of marketable cotton. One plantation owner said that his cotton-growing troubles would be eliminated if someone could invent a new machine to facilitate the process of detaching the green cotton seed.

Eli's hosts had observed Whitney's ingenuity with tools and suggested that he turn his attention to the problem. Within ten days Whitney had designed a model of the cotton gin. This simple hand-cranked device separated the cotton fiber from the green seeds of upland cotton. By April 1793 he had built an improved machine that enabled one person to produce fifty pounds of cleaned cotton in a day.

In 1795, the year after Whitney patented his cotton gin, cotton exports soared from a previous annual average of less than two hundred thousand pounds to over six million pounds. By revolutionizing cotton production for Southern plantations at the turn of the nineteenth-century, Whitney secured the destiny of Savannah throughout the 1800s. As Georgia's principal port, Savannah became the primary outlet for exporting Southern cotton overseas.

As the center of commercial trading in Georgia before the Civil War, the Savannah Cotton Exchange was once the Mecca for the cotton merchants of the South as the world's foremost cotton port.

SAVANNAH, *Southern Survivor*

branches, which boosted economic status for the city. For added security, the United States built and manned two forts in the 1830s to protect the strategic port as part of its coastal defense plan.

Funded by city and state public works appropriations, Savannah experienced expansive urban renewal projects in the 1840s. Gas lines were laid under the city's streets, and antiquated oil lamps were replaced with modern gas street lamps. Sunken wrecks that had obstructed the city harbor since the Revolutionary War were removed, and the previously deep river channels were dredged, which improved maritime approach to the docks and wharves.

Because of its access to the Atlantic, Savannah gained significance earlier than most Victorian towns. With Savannah's routes to the sea restored, investors such as The Central Railroad Banking Company began construction of a railroad line to link inland agricultural suppliers with coastal distributors. Since 1815, steamboats had traveled the Savannah River from eastern Georgia, but as the state's cotton plantations quickly developed after the invention of the cotton gin, upstate growers needed more efficient means for transporting their crops.

The Central of Georgia Railroad was conceived, financed, and constructed by local entrepreneurs in conjunction with the City of Savannah. The railroad line to Macon was completed in 1843, which allowed cotton growers a fast, cost-effective method for delivering large harvests to waterfront brokers. Following the completion of the new railroad network, annual Georgia cotton exports dramatically grew by a hundred thousand bales in just one decade.

Improvements in trade and transportation allowed Savannah to prosper and grow in the 1850s. The city population had doubled to fifteen thousand in less than one generation, and many of the new town arrivals were successful families that built fashionable homes and contributed to civic improvement funds. The original ward squares were adorned with historical monuments, and an expansive central city park with fountains and promenades was landscaped.

As community pride flourished, public and private institutions evolved. The Baptist and Methodist churches attracted large congregations, and the First African Baptist Church, organized in 1788, erected a brick worship hall in the 1850s. Church structures outnumbered school buildings in ante-bellum Savannah, and religion, education, and tradition were reflected in the architecture, culture, and lifestyle of the mid-nineteenth-century port city.

In 1855, Savannah epitomized the idyllic, peaceful Southern river town. An earlier settler described the town this way:

Known as "The Lord of LaFayette Square," merchant mogul S.P. Hamilton ordered a sumptuous and commodious house to be erected on the southeast quadrant of LaFayette Square at a cost of one hundred thousand dollars in 1873. Hamilton's home became a social landmark, where countless cotillions, debuts, weddings, and receptions were held.

SAVANNAH, *Southern Survivor*

Left: **This home, built in 1892, combines a Queen Anne tower with Gothic arches to create a hybrid example that illustrates Savannah's eclectic blend of Victorian structures.**

Right: **Since fire was a constant threat in towns like Savannah, the use of brick was encouraged for both residential and commercial buildings. The peak of this building illustrates the dimensional effects created by using brickwork in various patterns and colors.**

"a tranquil old city, wide-streeted, tree-planted with a few cows and carriages toiling through the sandy roads, a few happy Negroes sauntering here and there, a red river with a contented little fleet of merchantmen taking in cargo, warehouses barricaded with packs of cotton, no tearing Northern hustle, no ceaseless hotel racket, no crowds."

Because of commercial development in the 1850s, however, Savannah began to outgrow its Southern provincial lifestyle. By 1856, the original "commons area" had been developed into twenty-four city wards, and the success from the cotton trade led to diversification in the local economy. By 1860, manufacturing businesses contributed over two million dollars worth of annual profits from finished goods to Savannah investors.

For several years, business boomed in Savannah, but the political turmoil between the North and the South threatened the port city's financial future. With the outbreak of the Civil War, Union forces interrupted all maritime export activity by blockading the mouth of the Savannah River. This naval siege lasted throughout the war and left the trade-dependent economy paralyzed; many under-capitalized local businesses declared bankruptcy.

By 1864, Savannah had succumbed to

Georgia was the fifth state to secede from the Union and join the Confederacy in January of 1861. During the Civil War, the Port of Savannah was blockaded by federal warships, and the local economy suffered immeasurably. After the war, Georgia was readmitted to the Union in 1870, but Savannah never regained its supremacy as the principal trading port along the southern Atlantic seaboard.

As Georgia's oldest city, historic Savannah has endured wars and fires since it was settled in 1733 to become an eclectic mixture of colonial, antebellum, and Victorian architecture. Riverfront Savannah remains much the way its founder and planner, James Oglethorpe, envisioned the city: a grid-like pattern of neighborhoods interspersed with public parks. Savannah's growth as a port and shipping center was determined by its strategic location on open, level ground — the savannah — above its accessible river and harbor.

Military action during the Revolutionary War and a fire in 1796 destroyed many wooden Colonial buildings. Fifteen years after Savannah was rebuilt, defenses were erected around the town during the War of 1812, and the city averted attack and damage by British forces. The great fire of 1825, however, burned almost five hundred buildings.

As Georgia's thriving cotton plantation's brought trade and prosperity to Savannah, skilled architects and craftsmen produced "a showy little city," as one English visitor described it. After the devastation of previous fires, elegant residences were constructed of large porous bricks known as "Savannah grays" that were fired in kilns beside the river. Ornamental ironwork cast into balconies, railings, gates, and spires and were added prolifically to houses. On the eve of the Civil War, Savannah encompassed twenty-four squares with tranquil, wooded parks.

When General Sherman's Union Army invaded Georgia in 1864 and laid siege to Atlanta, Savannah lost its valuable cotton trade. Atlanta fell on September 2, and when Sherman left the city on November 16, it was burned to the ground. Sherman's soldiers began their "March to the Sea," cutting a fifty-mile swath of scorched earth across the state. They reached Savannah on December 21, and the city surrendered without a fight. Sherman spared the strategic port as "a Christmas gift" for his commander-in-chief, President Lincoln.

After the Civil War the Reconstruction era was less harsh in Georgia than in other Southern states, but the economy was in ruins. Slaves were freed, and money to hire labor was unavailable. The cotton plantations were broken into small plots, and the inefficient system of tenancy and sharecropping was instituted.

The boundless outlook that Savannahians had acquired in their days of opulence did not survive into Reconstruction. The characteristic gray brick buildings lost precedence when the last riverside kiln closed in the 1880s. Nevertheless, many elegant Victorian residences were built during the Reconstruction era by businessmen and war heroes who had the financial resources to construct fashionable new homes in Savannah's postwar neighborhoods. Victorian architectural styles superseded the Greek Revival, Gothic, and Romanesque motifs that were used before the war.

As a result, Savannah evolved into a city with various architectural styles. From the original city plans of Oglethorpe, the town acquired a colonial formality and order that is apparent in its geometric gridwork of streets and parks. From the opulent "Golden Age" when cotton trade flourished, there is an ostentatious flair to the cast-iron ornamentation that embellishes most of the city's antebellum architecture. Finally, from the building renaissance that rejuvenated Savannah during the Reconstruction era, there is the unmistakable presence of Victorian innovation that allowed for experimentation and progress towards novel architecture. Clearly, Savannah reflects a mixture of influences that has shaped and defined its character.

Left: **This brickwork facade displays an elaborate frieze in varying patterns, which embellishes the tower and wall at various levels.**

Right: **This Romanesque home was designed by W.G. Preston in 1889 for George Baldwin, one of Savannah's best known and most public-spirited citizens. He was the founder of many civic groups and sat on the boards of over two dozen local organizations. He introduced trolley cars to Savannah for public transportation and helped to organize the Custom House, Cotton Exchange, and Port of Savannah.**

Left: **This notable Savannah landmark is known as The Gingerbread House. Built in 1899 by Cord Asendorf, a prosperous German-born grocer, this delightful Victorian has been restored inside-and-out to provide local groups with a unique venue for holding special events and celebrations.**

Right: **A buzzword of Victorian terminology, "gingerbread," is translated from a medieval French word, gingimbrat, meaning "preserved ginger"; the British aristocracy borrowed the term to describe ginger-flavored cake, cut in fancy shapes. The expression was figuratively used in eighteenth-century England to describe ornate wooden fretwork, and the term eventually gained popularity in America as well.**

SAVANNAH, *Southern Survivor*

the isolation of war, and Union General William Sherman marched his soldiers across Georgia toward the sea to claim his prize. To spare their beloved city from total military destruction, Savannah's leaders quietly surrendered control to Sherman in December. The general then sent his famous telegram to President Lincoln, stating, "I beg to present to you, Mr. President, as a Christmas gift, the City of Savannah."

After the Civil War, Savannah attempted to regain its lost momentum as a vital trade center. The political uncertainties of Reconstruction, however, stifled new investment by outsiders, and local businessmen were either broke or heavily in debt. Cotton production had increased despite the war, but prices had dropped due to newer, more efficient cotton growing areas in the Southwest.

Cotton exports, which had propelled the Savannah economy before the war, faced an uncertain future. The once-rich Georgia soil had been over-farmed and depleted of minerals, and the dreaded boll weevil began to cut an eastward path of crop devastation in the South. Upstate cotton planters who previously shipped their harvests to Savannah left Georgia to search for farming opportunities in the West.

In the late nineteenth-century, Savannah sought new economic growth with a diversified industrial and agricultural base. Some factories were built with the help of Northern capital, but many Georgians mistrusted outside investment and chose to return to an agrarian lifestyle. Attempts were made to grow peaches, pecans, peanuts, corn, and tobacco, but most farmers, hoping to supply the area's floundering textile industry, stubbornly continued to grow cotton.

By 1920, the cotton economy had collapsed, and Savannah, which had failed to diversify in over fifty years, slid into mediocrity. The original mansions and inspirational homes of the Victorian Era were abandoned for repetitious row houses and unimaginative apartments. The elegance and frivolity of Savannah's nineteenth-century architecture were forsaken for unemotional, mundane, concrete-slab designs based on mass production and cost-cutting.

A second cityscape emerged from this dubious building trend, obscuring Savannah's Victorian houses. New buildings sprang up near suburban highways and freeways, with shiny facades of metal and glass that reflected a postwar architectural penchant for modern minimalism. In the shadows of these trendy towers remain a few pockets of historical heritage, where downtown homeowners have kept traditional architecture alive amidst the burned-out, boarded-up buildings.

For the past several decades local preservationists have been working hard to salvage these older neighborhoods and convert them into architecturally protected districts. With the help of the Georgia Historical Society, local business people, and volunteer donations, several vintage houses have been purchased for renovation and display as educational tour sites. One such building houses a museum and headquarters for Historic Savannah.

Today Historic Savannah is actively involved in sharing this city's glorious architecture and history with thousands of visitors each year. Educational exhibits are displayed for the public and knowledgeable guides offer theme tours through many of Savannah's most significant homes and neighborhoods. Savannah has endured the passage of war, pestilence, and disease to earn its title among Victorian enthusiasts as the "Southern Survivor."

Savannah's former opulence is reflected in the City Hall's gilded dome, a classic form that symbolically represents power and justice. The domed roof, considered by architectural historians to be a variation of the church steeple, has represented religious and secular authority for centuries in European cultures. Architects in America often used traditional forms to design their Victorian and neoclassical buildings.

Left: **Magnolia Place, built in 1883, was the home of Jacob Heyward, a career sea captain who sailed for the Confederacy during the Civil War and was captured and imprisoned by the Yankees. After the war, Captain Heyward designed an elegant retirement home in Savannah, where he claimed the winds were laden with the tang of salt water. Over the years, Magnolia Place hosted many social events, where young blades sought the favor of the city's Southern belles. Today, Heyward's home has been impeccably restored and currently reigns as the gracious Grand Inn of Savannah, Magnolia Place.**

Right: **This fountain serves as the focal point of Forsyth Park, a promenade once used by the social elite for walks with wealthy, expensively dressed children led by nursemaids for inspection by Savannah's important citizens. The design for this fountain took first prize in London at an international exhibition in 1851. Castings were sent to a European city, where a duplicate of Savannah's fountain still cascades in the town plaza against the backdrop of Baroque buildings.**

SAVANNAH, *Southern Survivor*

EUREKA SPRINGS

The City That Water Built

*Left: **This outdoor mural, which decorates the entire side of a building in the Historic District of Eureka Springs, pictorially traces the area's history during the nineteenth-century, and it was commissioned by civic leaders to commemorate the town's centennial anniversary.***

*Right: **Trolleys, which were the only practical means of public transportation for negotiating the hills of Eureka Springs before the turn of the century, again provide convenient access from the hillside residences to the historic business and shopping areas of town.***

For centuries the Osage Indians of the Midwestern plains had visited a place they called "the great healing Spring of the Arkansas." During hunting trips these tribes traveled hundreds of miles from the prairies to rejuvenate themselves at the mineral springs in the Ozarks, which offered legendary curative powers. The Sioux Indians of the Great Lakes region tell a tribal story about how a great Chieftain's daughter, born with a blinding illness, had her eyesight restored by the medicinal powers of the spring waters.

Dr. Alvah Jackson heard about the Indian legends and explored the Ozark wilderness in search of the magical springs, which he located in 1856. He established his practice in nearby Carroll County where he began to treat his patients with what he termed "the medical virtues in the water." In the 1860s Dr. Jackson bottled the spring water and traveled around the country to treat a variety of afflictions, including the wounds of Civil War soldiers.

News of the miraculous water brought hundreds of health seekers to its source at "Eureka Springs," a name attributed to the first enthusiasts who found inspiration at the basin-shaped cavity along a solitary escarpment. By 1879, over four hundred visitors formed a tent settlement around the springs in which they placed their hope for salvation from a multitude of diseases, ailments, and chronic illnesses. Many desperately ill individuals ominously arrived only with a single valise carrying their "buryin' clothes."

Naturally where there were plenty of patients, droves of "doctors" soon arrived to supervise the spa activities. Temporary tent sites were soon replaced by more permanent structures as their patients grew in numbers. Taverns sprang up to satisfy the thirst of those seeking more powerful potions. Basin ("Eureka") Spring became the center of the new town, where the first public bathhouse was constructed in a cluster of buildings next to a grocery store, boarding house, and hardware dealer.

In August 1879 the townspeople elected a governing body, which began to survey the town for the construction of streets. The first explorers reached the springs individually on horseback, but as hundreds of families came to resettle in

Left: Before building this home, Powell Clayton owned a Southern plantation with his brother, until the Civil War divided their family and turned the brothers into enemies.

Right: Powell Clayton served in the Union Army during the Civil War, and he was mustered out as a brigadier general. He became the first "carpet-bag" governor of Arkansas during Reconstruction. After losing his reelection campaign, Clayton moved his family to Eureka Springs and built this home in 1881. As one of the town's most influential citizens, he was an advocate of "city planning" and helped to modernize the town's public utilities and transportation systems.

carriages and wagons filled with household belongings, improved roads leading to homesites were in immediate demand. Trees were cut in great numbers to provide building sites and materials, and by the end of 1879 fifteen hundred lots had been surveyed for development.

Hundreds of simple frame buildings were hastily constructed to house the rapid influx of population. On February 14, 1880, the town became incorporated, with an estimated three thousand permanent residents as well as fifteen thousand annual visitors. With sixty-three active springs within the town limits, crowds of faithful bathers frequented the growing number of bathhouses and hotels to indulge in the waters.

In the 1880s people from all backgrounds were attracted to Eureka Springs. They brought with them a demand for creature comforts and cultural propriety. The main streets were lined with shops that showcased the latest in housewares, stylish clothing, and even local souvenirs. Several religious denominations were organized, and over fifteen hundred children were taught by educators in a dozen locations around town.

As the reputation of Eureka Springs increased, regional newspapers featured remarkable testimonials by residents who claimed to have been revitalized by the springs. Daily mail service was established to link locally resettled families with their hometown friends and relatives. The reports spread that Eureka Springs had grown from a simple encampment of desperate sufferers to become an extravagant spa resort town with over thirty elegant hotels.

The commercial prosperity of Eureka Springs brought new wealth to its entrepreneurs, who began to replace their simple frame dwellings with impressive Victorian structures. Many of these founding families built new homes along the residential upper ridges with commanding views of the town center in the valley. Steep stairways of breathless flights were built into the hills to connect elevated homes and hotels to businesses below.

By 1882 Eureka Springs had become the fourth largest city in the state of Arkansas. Stagecoach lines, which carried over a hundred passengers per day to the town during a dusty nine-hour journey from the railhead at Pierce City, Missouri, were a considerable inconvenience to affluent travelers. Increased demand for better transportation led to the construction of the Eureka Springs Railroad in 1883, which was connected with the Frisco Line at Seligman, Missouri to provide direct passenger service to the springs.

The Frisco Company capitalized on the novelty of their new direct railroad

The exterior of this fifteen-room house is painted brick red, cream, maroon, and green to duplicate the original palette revealed through preliminary paint scrapings. J.W. Hill, the wealthiest bachelor in town, built the Rosalie in 1883 for seventeen thousand dollars. Mr. Hill installed the first private telephone system in town to conduct business between his Tallyho's Freight Transfer Company and Crescent Livery Stables.

EUREKA SPRINGS, *The City That Water Built*

81

connection to Eureka Springs by advertising Pullman sleeping cars, elegant dining cars, and complimentary Basin Spring water served to all passengers. Soon six trains a day carried eager travelers to the accessible resort town. Arrivals were met at the train depot by handsome horse-drawn carriages and "tallyhos," which whisked guests away to luxurious hotel accommodations.

Like many booming Victorian towns, Eureka Springs, in its eagerness to capitalize on unbridled growth, fell victim to a common fatal force — fire. In November 1883 the first of four extensive fires ravaged large portions of the city by racing up its steep wooded hills and decimating seventy-five structures before the volunteer "Bucket Brigade" could halt its devastation. Undaunted, the townspeople quickly rebuilt their wooden Victorian homes, and in a gesture tempting fate, added gas-powered streetlights as well.

Rapid progress continued in the 1890s as Eureka Springs flourished with tourism and economic growth. A municipal water system was finished in 1894 that supplied all local businesses and residences with the town's famous water. Telephones were first installed in 1895 by a visionary entrepreneur who anticipated the need for communication between the relatively isolated locations upon the town's foothills. The intimidating inclines of Eureka Springs

TESTIMONIAL

In a place where so many with afflictions became cured, testimonials flourished among local gossipers. Everybody had a high stake in cures, either to bolster their own faith or perhaps to convince someone else that they too would be healed. In the naive arena of faithful optimism that surrounded Eureka Springs, a rumor easily earned the respect of a hard fact.

A booklet published in 1881 offered the following testimonials about local health seekers who had benefited from the curative powers of the springs: "Miss Frances Bell, of Harrison, Boone County, Arkansas, came here last February, afflicted with paralysis; could not walk a step, or even stand — was perfectly helpless. Now she says she is entirely cured; can walk around over Eureka Hills without any trouble." The same publication also described a "John W. McVey with 'scrofula,' twenty years; sore eyes of two years; loss of sight in left eye, nine months before coming to the Springs, from inflammation. In five weeks could read with the blind eye; sores and ulcers all healed. His stay, three months; used Eureka, Johnson, and Oil waters." Testimonials like these were inspirational to others, who waited for their own miraculous salvation by "The City That Water Built."

After a hiatus of over half a century, steam trains again whistle in Eureka Springs. This working collection of vintage steam engines and passenger cars is an authentic re-creation of the ES & NA railroad that brought thousands of visitors to experience the area's curative mineral springs over a hundred years ago.

Left: **The description of this house in the Daily Times-Echo newspaper in 1906 read, "Cozy Corners is one of the prettiest properties of the city, and it is owned by Dr. A.E. and Dr. Pearl Tatman. This enterprising couple, besides enjoying a large practice, own their own substantial stone office building." Pearl Tatman is still fondly remembered in the community, and she lived in this home until the 1940s.**

Right: **Contractor and builder W.O. Perkins is credited with the construction of this house in the 1890s, as well as many other homes in Eureka Springs. He enjoyed a long and successful career, and this detail view illustrates the finesse of his skills.**

were conquered first by horse-drawn trolleys in 1891, which were replaced by an electric streetcar system in 1899.

Because most of the town was precariously built along two steep ridges, the engineers of Eureka Springs took extraordinary measures to fortify their roads and buildings against landslides due to floods and erosion. In 1892, all principal streets were graded and widened to improve their utility. By the turn of the century over fifty miles of native stone retaining walls had been built to maintain the curved upper roads and prevent rainy mud slides.

With its glorious architecture, splendid transportation, and an insatiable demand for its healing waters, Eureka Springs thrived for over two decades as a premier resort town. Visitors came to spend their time and money with carefree optimism, investing their livelihood with the hedonistic indulgence of devotees seeking the fountain of youth. The zealous attitude of the faithful was positively contagious as they pursued personal tranquillity and health.

Tourists swarmed local shops to purchase souvenirs of local onyx, hand-carved walking sticks, and of course bottles of the famous water. Days were spent hiking the rough terrain in fresh mountain air, soaking in the invigorating spring waters, and enjoying freshly-packed picnic lunches.

This house was probably built in the mid-1890s as one of a pair of "elegant cottages." In 1923, the Woman's Missionary Society purchased this home with money raised by giving fund raising dinners in the home, twice monthly, for over a year. Later the building was deeded to the Methodist Church to be used as a parsonage, and it continues to house the minister for their local congregation to this day.

Concert bands performed daily at the Basin Spring Pavilion during the summer, and evening entertainment included literary readings, theatrical productions, and grand musicales staged in the splendid hotel ballrooms.

By the turn of the century, however, the therapeutic waters of Eureka Springs were superseded by the introduction of more modern medicines, and many visitors replaced their sojourns to the spa with visits to the local pharmacy. Their reliance and faith in natural cures were replaced by new potions in the medicine chest, which brought health care back into the home and deterred people from visiting distant hotels. In just a few years, the popularity of Eureka Springs as a health resort dropped dramatically.

Civic leaders became distressed and looked for ways to modernize the image of Eureka Springs. Some residents expected the popular new automobile to bring another wave of visitors to their town, and a dozen more progressive citizens purchased the newfangled vehicles to test the safety of the winding streets in their neighborhoods. But the invention of the family car was no substitute for the miracle cures of medicine, and travelers lost interest in Eureka Springs as a destination.

By 1916 the town's population had diminished to less than three thousand residents. The once-fashionable resort hotels closed and fell into disrepair. Transportation business floundered, and both passenger railway services to Eureka Springs and streetcar operation within the town were terminated. As the Great Depression paralyzed the economy, Eureka Springs became frozen in time and did not thaw the freeze of forsaken neglect for several decades.

Like many forgotten towns of a different era, Eureka Springs was eventually rediscovered in the 1960s by a new generation of enthusiasts. Artists were attracted to the undisturbed creative energy of the area; spiritual leaders made pilgrimages to purify themselves in the springs. Vacationers saw the Ozarks as an unpretentious place to relax, and they were delighted to encounter this picturesque Victorian village nestled in the Arkansas hills.

By 1970 craftspeople, artists, and collectors began to open quaint shops and galleries along the steep stairways and winding streets that twisted up the slopes of Eureka Springs. In 1972 local preservationists petitioned and received approval to declare the original town limits a National Historic District. In 1979 the Centennial Mural was painted by local artists on the side of a downtown building to commemorate a century of local history.

Disillusioned urbanites returned to the

Left: **W.O. Perkins, whose fine craftsmanship is exemplified in these brace supports, gained an outstanding reputation as a builder in Eureka Springs for his trademark usage of intricate textures and patterns.**

Right: **This home was built by W.O. Perkins in 1886 as a honeymoon home for Dr. C.F. Ellis, who came to Eureka Springs shortly after its inception and became one of the town's most prominent physicians.**

friendly town in the 1980s to raise their families while restoring the original status of their vintage homes. Many Victorian houses were renovated and converted into country inns, which now draw increased crowds of guests and visitors on the weekends. The fall season is especially popular with visitors, who come to enjoy the town's vivid atmosphere as its graceful trees shower the hillsides with a cornucopia of colors.

Today Eureka Springs bustles with diverse activity from historical home tours, hundreds of specialty shops and galleries, and the phenomenal Passion Play, which is performed outdoors by an epic cast of actors and animals each evening during the summer months. Replicated trolleys traverse the elevated neighborhoods for the convenience of grateful pedestrians. The steam trains that originally carried nineteenth-century passengers have been retooled and follow new tracks along the valley for local excursions. "The City That Water Built" has washed its memories, polished its past, and sparkles with an effervescent vitality that animates its unique history.

Carry A. Nation, one of American history's most controversial women, dedicated her public life to moral reform, but her personal life was plagued by emotional turmoil. Carry married a young physician addicted to alcohol and attempted to reform him. Her efforts were unsuccesful and she left him only to find he died of alcolholism six months later. After the loss of her first spouse, Carry moved to Kansas where she married a lawyer and minister named David Nation. It was a strange relationship that ended with her spouse divorcing her for desertion.

Kansas was one of the original prohibition states, and despite stringent enforcement, there were numerous "joints" where liquor was sold. Carry organized a branch of the Woman's Christian Temperance Union, whose members began to raid illicit bars and expel the "jointists." They argued that it was justifiable for righteous citizens to forcibly destroy not only liquor, but also furniture and fixtures in saloons, since serving alcohol was illegal in Kansas. Such property, Carry avowed, "has no rights that anybody is bound to respect."

A commanding woman at six feet tall, she dramatized her protest against illegal saloons in Kansas by wrecking the saloon in Wichita's Hotel Carey with a hatchet, a distinctive weapon that became her symbolic trademark. Carry continued on her rampage throughout the country, and authorities arrested her over thirty times — usually on charges of "disturbing the peace." She paid her numerous fines with earnings made from the sale of souvenir hatchets, lecture tours, and stage appearances. She never became wealthy, but her popularity continued to finance her crusades for many years.

Increasing feebleness forced Carry's retirement to Eureka Springs, where she named her home "Hatchet Hall" in honor of the weapon she had wielded against alcohol; there she ran a boarding house for families of alcoholics until her death. Throughout her life Carry claimed to have personal mystical experiences, including the vision of a spring near her home. She asked that the rocky wall across from her house be excavated, which indeed revealed a spring within a large cave. The spring supplied nearby homes with fresh, cool water, and the cave also served as a natural refrigerator for her friends' perishable food items.

By the time a constitutional amendment prohibiting alcohol was enacted by Congress in 1920, Carry A. Nation had been overshadowed by a new generation of salvationists. Her personal activism and foresight with the concerns of alcoholism inspired others to carry her cause to its successful completion. The inscription on the monument at her grave site says simply, "She hath done what she could."

This hand-carved sunburst pattern on the gable of the local Presbyterian Manse was documented in a book published in 1881 as one of the town's "oldest ornamented structures." Most of Eureka Springs' best examples of traditional Victorian residences are found along this section of Spring Street.

Left: **This Tiffany-designed Wisteria Lamp, prominently displayed in the Queen Anne Mansion, was made by a protege and former associate of Louis Comfort Tiffany.**

Right: *A seemingly impossible task was undertaken when the new owners of this mansion bought the stone building in another state with the intention of moving the structure, piece by piece, to Eureka Springs. The home was originally built in Carthage, Missouri in 1891 at a cost of twenty-one thousand five hundred dollars. For the move, every piece was numbered, charted, individually transported, and reassembled on its present site.*

94

GALVESTON

Island in Time

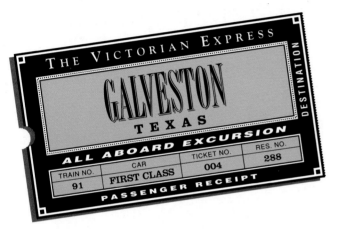

The Elissa, *a sailing ship built in 1887, is anchored in Galveston's harbor and serves as a maritime museum as well as a training vessel.*

alveston, Texas, located on a remote island along the Gulf of Mexico, has been both blessed and cursed by its geographical isolation. A variety of Indians, explorers, pirates, slaves, speculators, journalists, immigrants, missionaries, minstels, medicine men, educators, prostitutes, smugglers, gangsters, gamblers, Yankees and Confederates have all contributed to Galveston's colorful history. After almost two centuries of competition, corruption, and coastal calamities, success and failure have recurrently swayed Galveston's pendulum of destiny.

The stretch of land that eventually became the foundation for Galveston virtually grew from the sea. As the ocean that had flooded the coastal inland receded, it left behind a sand bar that trapped silt and debris, forming a barrier island twenty-seven miles long and three miles wide. Reptiles, rodents, and insects migrated to the dunes and estuaries, while the wind and sea birds transported the first seeds for vegetation to the island's shores.

Nomadic Indians called the Karankawas seasonally roamed the Texas and Louisiana coastal region during low tides in search of food. They fished the shallow inlet waters, gathered oysters and shellfish, and speared reptiles. Reputedly these primitive tribes would smother their bodies in alligator grease to repel insects while performing cannibalistic rituals such as offering human flesh for sacrifice.

During the late 1700s, European explorers from the Netherlands, France, and Spain traversed the Gulf Coast, seeking safe anchorage from the frequent tropical storms that blew up from the Caribbean. In 1785, José Evia surveyed the area for the Spanish Governor of Louisiana, Count Bernardo de Galvez. Evia discovered a secluded bay, which he named in honor of Galvez, although it is unlikely that the Count ever visited his namesake.

Until the nineteenth-century, the Isle de Galvez was uninhabited except for an occasional fugitive from justice, who usually fell victim to the thousands of rattlesnakes that occupied the forsaken island. The area's sole attraction was a deep harbor accessible only by a secret channel lying amidst shallow shoal waters. This hidden haven appealed to privateers and pirates who ambushed passing treasure-laden ships of the Spanish Crown.

The Mexican governor of Texas commissioned a French mercenary in 1816 to establish a permanent settlement near the harbor. Mexico hoped to obtain a strategic port on the Gulf for launching attacks against towns and ships loyal to the Spanish royalty. Besides the harassment from Mexican opportunists, the Spanish cargo ships were also plundered by a band of notorious pirates led by the infamous Jean Lafitte.

Lafitte's group of incorrigibles seized the lightly fortified island settlement in 1817 and named it "Campeche." The pirate encampment grew to over two thousand inhabitants during the next four years, as smuggling, slave trading, and the sale of captured cargo fostered a flourishing black market economy. When one of Lafitte's captains seized an American vessel, however, he drew the wrath of the United States Navy, which demanded a complete evacuation of Lafitte's village by May of 1821.

Sunflower designs found their roots in English Queen Anne architecture and remained in vogue for many years. Early Victorian architects who used this style were admirers of Classical poetry that vividly described these bright flowers. The sunflower motif used here embellishes the steep roof gables, creating a different facade on each elevation.

Right: The owner of this Queen Anne home, a lumber merchant and banker, personally supervised its design and construction in 1889. The home's unusual corner entrance, use of patterned shingles, and highly ornamented gables were combined to individualize this vibrant Victorian.

Left: **Endless variations of faces, flowers, and forms were included in the intricately carved details that appeared in exterior arabesques. The ship's wheel design within the arches of this Galveston balcony reflects the port town's early maritime history.**

Right: **This home, completed in 1890, provided safe shelter for neighborhood families during the Storm of 1900. Fourteen live oak trees, now over ninety years old, were planted to replace the trees and shrubbery lost in the storm.**

Faced with the impending approach of American warships, Lafitte unveiled a bountiful supply of wine and whiskey in his cellar and threw an unabashed orgy for his decadent followers. He then ordered his ships loaded with contraband, torched the settlement's buildings, and sailed away for ports unknown. After Lafitte's departure, wishful scavengers scoured the island in search of buried treasure, but years of excavation revealed only a few doubloons and indigenous artifacts.

By 1825 the Texas territory had become a burden for the Mexican government. It did not have the national resources or population to resettle the region north of the Rio Grande, so it entered into desperate agreements with American speculators. A loophole in the Mexican Colonization Law allowed Americans to act as "agents" for Mexican landholders. A group of ten American businessmen thereby negotiated the purchase of the island from Mexico for fifty-thousand dollars and formed a development firm they called the Galveston City Company.

In the 1830s an influx of immigrants landed in "Galveztown." This first colony of settlers pitched tents on the ruins of the pirate village, opened shops in crude huts, and utilized a shipwrecked brigantine as a temporary shelter for visitors. In his travel journal, John James Audubon, the famous

The ship's wheel design in the balustrade of this wedding cottage seemed to indicate Brown's approval of his new son-in law's maritime business, but the property was deeded only to Matilda, his daughter.

Right: **As a wedding gift to his daughter Matilda, James Brown of Ashton Villa** *had this home built* **in 1885 within sight on his own residence. The** *design of this "wedding cottage" is attributed to Nicholas Clayton, Galveston's most prolific architect in the nineteenth-century.*

GAIL BORDEN

ail Borden, as an inventor, entrepreneur, and humanitarian epitomized the architypal Victorian man. Born as the son of a poor farmer, Borden received little formal education during childhood. Gail struggled as a self-disciplined teenager to excel in gunmanship and teach himself surveying. Plagued by poor health as a young man, he left his inland home to recuperate along the sunny Texas coast where he met many land speculators.

With the help of eight real estate investors he created a land development firm called the Galveston City Company. Borden and his partners purchased an island on the Gulf Coast from Mexico in 1825 for fifty-thousand dollars. During the following decade he surveyed their island and laid out the first city plans for Galveston. From 1838 to 1851, Borden built the Galveston City Company into a powerful and profitable corporation that owned, developed, and leased the majority of residential and commercial properties in Galveston.

As a self-made millionaire, Borden began his most important work in the field of nutrition. As a pioneer surveyor, he personally experienced the hardship of securing and carrying sufficient unspoiled food while camped in the wilderness. Borden sought to preserve different foods in concentrated forms. He first developed a dehydrated meat biscuit that seemed ideal for the military, so he invested his fortune in a manufacturing plant. Political interference by Army food contractors, however, prevented the distribution of his invention, and Borden closed his business. Eventually Borden's competitors exploited his processing techniques and successfully supplied canned foods to the military during the Civil War.

Nearly broke, but not broken, Borden traveled outside America to market his meat biscuit at the London Fair in 1851. During his return ocean crossing from Europe, Borden was distressed by the unhealthy plight of immigrant children aboard ship who were deprived of wholesome milk. He began experiments with condensing milk, and Borden received a patent in 1856 to exclusively distribute his dairy product. Borden's Condensed Milk became a nationally popular food source where fresh dairy supplies were unavailable.

Borden continued his experimental work on concentrating foods, juices, tea, coffee and cocoa. Women's magazines popularized these products through their advertising. By the end of the nineteenth-century a great variety of processed foods became staples in the Victorian diet, and the Borden name continues as a major purveyor in the food industry today.

ornithologist, recorded his impression of the settlement as "only a miserable collection of huts, a few war prisoners, several chickens, one pig, and a dog."

During the next decade tension increased between American pioneers of the Republic and Mexican loyalists. A provisional army led by Sam Houston challenged the Mexican soldiers for two years until the bloody climax of the war for independence in 1836. Thousands of Anglo-Americans who had rushed westward to avenge the battle of the Alamo defeated the Mexican army. The Texan Republic was formed, and the American territorial presence in Texas was dramatically affirmed.

After the Texan revolution Galveston's rustic appearance quickly changed. Although President Jackson was reluctant to acknowledge the sovereignty of the Texan Republic, Congress recognized the strategic value of Galveston and declared it an official port of entry in 1837. The harbor was considered one of the best points of inland access along the Gulf Coast, and with federal endorsement international maritime trade precipitated rapid development in the area.

Steamships arrived from New Orleans loaded with German immigrants who sought refuge and opportunity in the Southwest territory. Cotton from inland

The multicolored slate pattern, which remains visible on the tower to the right, once covered the entire roof of this home.

plantations was loaded on return trips for delivery to textile mills in the eastern United States and England. Importers and exporters solicited trading agreements with cargo ship captains who frequently stopped at the active port en route to destinations in the Gulf of Mexico.

By 1839 the City of Galveston became incorporated, and residential and commercial lots were sold to eager immigrants and entrepreneurs. The boulevard that ran parallel to the island's southern beachfront became known as "The Strand" (the German word for "beach"), where resort hotels and prestigious businesses began to locate. As wholesalers, cotton brokers, insurance companies, hardware dealers, paint suppliers, and dry goods' stores proliferated along the oceanfront avenue, The Strand grew to become the most profitable street in Texas.

The news of Galveston's success circulated quickly through the eighteen city newspapers that began publication between 1838 and 1842. Because of its relative isolation from the events of the United States and Europe, local readers depended heavily on their English and German newspapers for news of the world. Only one daily newspaper survived those first four years of cutthroat competition for readers, and today *The Galveston News*, founded over a hundred and fifty years ago, continues to report the news to Texans.

As business boomed for Galveston's developers during the 1840s, successful local families began to invest in religious, educational, and cultural improvements for their city. Parochial private schools were opened by the Catholic, Presbyterian, and Methodist churches for the more affluent families' children, but little effort was made to educate the poor immigrants' offspring. Consequently Galveston began to develop a class system that reflected the Southern attitudes of its civic leaders.

Like other cities in the South during the mid-1800s, a dichotomy of lifestyles unfolded in Galveston. Wealthy, white, upper-class families leisurely entertained each other at teas, receptions, and dinners held in their spacious homes, where slaves attended to their owners' household duties. Meanwhile the struggling, immigrant class amused itself with street minstrels, medicine men, and circus performers. These two classes only mingled during public events such as church socials and the Mardi Gras festival — celebrated annually in Galveston since 1856.

The most divisive issue for Galvestonians was slavery, which forced Texan citizens to choose between economic prosperity for the state and political loyalty to the Union. Because slave labor had made inland cotton competitively priced for

Left: **The ironwork fence surrounding Ashton Villa was shortened considerably in height by Galveston's grade-raising after the Great Storm of 1900. These unusual "corn harvest" finials adorn the tops of the gateposts.**

Right: **Ashton Villa, built in 1859, has a colorful history that features one of Galveston's most prominent families. It was the first home in town to have a telephone and electric lights and Ashton Villa was the setting for lavish social functions over several generations.**

export, Galveston thrived as an agricultural trade center. When the Constitution was amended in 1845 to forbid the American importation of African slaves, the cotton business suffered in the South.

A decade of controversial debate arose among state businessmen and political leaders about whether Texas should secede from the slave-free Union. By 1860, Southern towns like Galveston were clearly divided into camps of Unionists and Secessionists, with the majority of businessmen favoring continued slavery. When Texas ultimately announced secession from the Union on February 1, 1861, preparations were well underway by local Confederate groups in Galveston to form a militia in defense of their strategic harbor city.

Since civil war appeared inevitable, and Galveston's isolation from Confederate support made it vulnerable to Union attack, many affluent Texan families packed their personal belongings, locked their houses, and left the island for Houston and relatively safer inland areas of the state. After the war began, President Lincoln ordered the Union Navy to blockade and capture all major Southern ports. Galveston was placed under siege and initially surrendered to the Federal forces on October 5, 1862.

In a daring reprisal four months later, however, a fleet of Confederate ships under the cover of darkness captured the Yankee warship guarding the harbor and bombarded the Union's occupational forces until they surrendered Galveston Island the next day. The "Battle of Galveston" was a pivotal victory for the Confederacy, who continued to use the valuable port for supplying its soldiers with arms, ammunition, and medical supplies from European sympathizers, trading for inland cotton. The Union continued to operate an expensive naval blockade in the Texas Gulf that only marginally controlled the elusive Confederate smugglers.

As the war turned against the South, the isolation of Galveston took its toll on the port city. Union warships repeatedly bombarded the island in frustration, and many town structures were crippled by cannon balls. Loyal Confederate defenders suffered a lack of food, fuel, and supplies during the siege, and fence post bonfires were set to keep the soldiers warm at night. By the end of the war in 1865, the architectural splendor of Galveston had fallen into demise, and the "Queen City Of Texas" had lost its majesty.

The surviving families of the war returned to Galveston to rebuild their town. With the departure of slavery, Texan cotton growers depended more on laborsaving devices, which ultimately made their Southwest operations more productive, competitive, and profitable while the dreaded boll weevil infested the large plantations of the traditional Southeast. Postwar investment and expansive trade revived Galveston and provided the city with the opportunity and resources to rebuild itself.

During the next decade Galveston was elevated to preeminent civic status. Streets were widened and illuminated with gaslamps, parks were landscaped, and the public square was beautified. A public trolley system was purchased to transport island residents around the expanding city. Business districts were developed and over two thousand new residences were constructed. Palatial mansions designed by Galveston's most noted architect, Nicholas Clayton, graced the city's most exclusive neighborhoods.

By the 1880s Galveston had established itself as the world's leading cotton port, and it continued to successfully export Texas cotton for several decades. Wholesalers traded millions of dollars in raw commodities for finished goods, and Galveston became known as "The New York of the Gulf." Volume levels competed with those of the major trading centers such as Chicago and St. Louis. Galveston became the financial center of Texas, and many state banks and insurance companies were established by local investors.

Galveston's success had depended on its exclusive ability to transport and trade Texas' raw commodities to outside markets; this achievement inspired inland competition. Houston entrepreneurs began to dredge the Buffalo Bayou River to a depth that would allow ocean-going ships safe passage fifty miles upstream to a port that offered direct access to the Texas railroad lines. Meanwhile, The Galveston Wharf Company had earned the unpopular nickname among foreign shippers as the "Octopus of the Gulf" for the monopolistic rates it charged to transfer cargo from trains to ships at Galveston Harbor.

Galveston's accessible shipping location on the Gulf Coast also made it a prime target for tropical hurricanes. On September 8, 1900, a deadly storm crashed upon the port with wind velocities of over one hundred twenty miles per hour that flooded the entire city with drowning surf. The hurricane killed six thousand people and inflicted millions of dollars worth of property damage. Many uninsured businesses went

The dance pavilion in the Silk Stocking Historical District is yet another creation of the prolific Galveston architect Nicholas J. Clayton. This talented architect produced plans for more than two hundred twenty-five structures on the Island during his prestigious career.

Left: **Stained glass windows at stairwell landings provided light and assured privacy from outside observers as Victorian ladies lifted their long skirts to ascend the steep stairs.**

Right: **Historical accounts suggest that the fourteen thousand dollar construction expense for this home, built in 1888, drove the builder into bankruptcy. The lattice work trellis on the galleries effectively combined light, shadow and ventilation for comfortable seating during afternoon teas.**

GALVESTON'S WORST CALAMITIES

1837 Lethal hurricane sweeps across Galveston Island.

1839 Yellow fever strikes two hundred fifty out of one thousand residents.

1844 Yellow fever epidemic, death toll is four hundred out of three thousand.

1853 Another plague of yellow fever kills over five hundred victims.

1858 Yellow fever scourge consumes six hundred helpless people.

1867 The largest and last yellow fever epidemic claims twelve hundred souls.

1875 Major tropical storm sinks ships in the port of Galveston.

1885 Fire scorches forty city blocks to burn one third of the city.

1898 Oceanfront blaze incinerates several luxury hotels on The Strand.

1900 The Great Storm of September drowns over six thousand residents.

1915 Storm clears the Sea wall and causes four million dollars in damage.

1947 Ship explodes with ammonium nitrate killing five hundred local workers.

1961 Hurricane Carla paralyzes the city with flooded isolation.

1974 Galveston waterfront is decimated by cotton warehouse fires.

1976 Costliest fire in port history destroys cargoes of cotton and rice.

1977 Central Hotel in downtown is destroyed by fire, leaving eight dead.

1979 Tanker *Burmah Agate* burns, spills oil near Galveston for seventy-eight days.

1984 Oil spill off Louisiana ruins beaches for summer tourist season.

1990 Supertanker spills millions of gallons of oil off Galveston coast.

Romanesque Revival characteristics intermingle with this Queen Anne tower to create a crossover style.

bankrupt, and it took Galveston's survivors almost four years to remove the worst devastation.

In 1904, hundreds of workers began to rebuild Galveston in a way that would minimize the destructive impact of future hurricanes. City planners designed a sea wall seven miles long and seventeen feet high. Since the city sat only eight feet above sea level, civil engineers ambitiously decided to raise all structures an additional four feet! This monumental task was accomplished by lifting each building on industrial jacks while dredges poured clay beneath the foundations of every building in Galveston.

This massive civic project took over seven years to complete, and it required the addition of over ten million cubic yards of earth to the city's ground level. Pedestrians crossed the town on wooden scaffolds for

During the Great Storm of 1900, every house in the neighborhood except this stone mansion was destroyed. Designed in 1888 by Nicholas Clayton for Colonel Walter Gresham, this home stands as a testament to the success of its owner. Gresham, after serving in the Confederate forces, moved to Galveston, where he was active in many civic affairs, including the successful effort to open a deep-water harbor for Galveston with federal funding.

most of the decade while buildings were hoisted to their new elevation. Virtually every tree and bush in Galveston was replaced in the storm's aftermath to restore landscaping to the desert-like terrain.

Galveston prevailed over the ravages of natural disaster, but it failed to recapture its competitive position as a commercial port in the twentieth-century. By 1914 the Houston Ship Canal had opened for seagoing traffic. Unsympathetic shippers eagerly bypassed rebuilt Galveston to deal directly with inland Texas wholesalers, who offered less expensive access to the inland railroad network. Houston eclipsed its competition to become the new trade center for Texas, and Galveston never regained its stature as a key Gulf Coast port.

As trade and transportation declined in significance for Galveston, city leaders sought to diversify its economic base by introducing service-oriented institutions and businesses to the area. The University of Texas School of Medicine attracted eminent educators and researchers, and a major insurance company established its world headquarters in Galveston. The sandy white beaches that formed along the new sea wall became a popular tourist attraction. Oceanfront resorts sponsored national bathing beauty contests in the 1920s to attract East and West Coast visitors to the warm water and gentle surf of the Gulf Coast.

Galveston's resorts relied heavily on the sale of alcoholic beverages to attract summer crowds, and when Prohibition became law, rum-running from the Caribbean kept illicit hotel bars and their owners in business. As organized crime invaded Galveston, extravagant casinos and tantalizing bordellos attracted visitors eager to indulge their vices. For several decades the "port of pleasures" satisfied the sinful expectations of tourists until the Texas Rangers raided Galveston in 1957 and shut down the party.

The architecture of Galveston suffered during this decadent period. From the 1930s to the 1970s, many of the city's vintage buildings were fortified with monotonous brick walls and mundane asbestos siding. Local preservationists were distraught to see elegant buildings along The Strand being demolished and replaced by concrete block hotels. In 1973, relief came from The Moody Foundation and The Eliza and Harris Kempner Fund, which contributed financial support for historic renovation activities.

Today the Galveston Historical Society operates a series of tours, exhibits, and activities dedicated to the preservation and appreciation of historic Galveston. Architectural aficionados may board replicas of the trolleys that traversed the city a century ago and be transported to various historic districts and neighborhoods. Guided tours are provided at many distin-guished Victorian homes by knowledgeable society volunteers. Ship enthusiasts may explore the workings of the fully-restored barkentine, *Elissa*, which is moored within walking distance of the Society's museum and visitor center.

Galveston has endured the misfortune of weather, war, and waste to survive as a witness to its past. The fortitude of its residents is testimony to their strength and courage in the face of natural and social adversities. Despite geographic, economic, and cultural isolation, the City of Galveston has persevered to affirm its historical tradition as an "Island in Time."

Reminiscent of the original streetcars that offered service around Galveston in the early twentieth-century, the Galveston Island Trolley again transports passengers from the beachfront on the Gulf Coast to The Stand at the deep-water harbor.

The Brooks Memorial Fountain was built in the
Greek Revival style in 1930 as part of Marshall's
centennial celebration. The fountain was given
to the city by Mayor Harold C. Brooks, in memory
of his father.

MARSHALL

The Crossroads of Progress

arshall, Michigan, like many Victorian towns, began as a resting place for travelers in the wilderness. In the early 1800s pioneers left Detroit and followed the southeast course of the Kalamazoo River through treacherous swamplands to reach Chicago. This artery of travel, known historically as The Territorial Road, was used by settlers from New England who moved westward through New York and Michigan in search of new opportunities.

Sidney Ketchum, a land speculator from New York, immediately recognized the promise for a new townsite while exploring land located at the fork of Rice Creek and the Kalamazoo River. Ketchum, who had roamed the territory to find such an ideal location, realized the great potential for utilizing the area's fertile soil, smooth terrain, vast forests, and abundant water supply. He envisioned transforming the area's inexpensive, undeveloped land into a thriving community for transportation, trade, and Eastern resettlement.

This dynamic developer joined forces with two other enterprising young speculators, an engineer and a lawyer, to buy out the "floating claims" of a few scattered settlers on adjacent unsurveyed property. These acquisitions of land near the townsite secured real estate for the prospect of community access and residential growth. To enhance the image of his new settlement, Ketchum named the town after his hero, John Marshall, who was born in a humble log cabin and persevered to become a Supreme Court Chief Justice.

With this preliminary ground-work accomplished, Ketchum wrote to his brother in Rochester, New York, that he had found a new homesite for his family, and he asked George to help him recruit construction workmen and transport building equipment to Marshall. Sidney

Left: **Brackets with rich detailing frequently embellished Italian Villa homes. By the 1860s, mills with steam-powered machines for making doors, window frames and moldings were built near many small American cities and villages like Marshall.**

Right: **The original owner of this home, built in 1870, was a proprietor of a crockery store, and its stock included: "glass, plated-ware, Ohio stoneware, zinc, toiletware, mirrors, table cutlery, toys, bird cages, perfumery, chandeliers and lamp goods of every description." This home has had only three different owners over the past one hundred twenty years.**

then returned to New York to help his parents, wife, five children, and a sister prepare for their trip to Michigan. The Ketchum family arrived to establish Marshall in July of 1831.

Since Marshall marked the halfway point between Detroit and Chicago, the Ketchums hoped that travelers on The Territorial Road would stop at their town to recuperate. Arrivals first came to Marshall by horseback; then more passengers followed by stagecoach, which created a growing demand for overnight accommodations in town. From its inception, Marshall gained quick popularity among weary riders as a welcome location for food and lodging.

Transportation improvements such as the completion of the Erie Canal increased the number of travelers willing to venture west of New York, despite the pessimistic reports by Andrew Jackson's official surveyor that, "Not one acre in a hundred would be arable." Soon the pioneer settlement of Marshall was bustling with activity, as New England families arrived from Vermont, Massachusetts, and New Hampshire to establish their new homes. Michigan, which had achieved little notoriety during the early nineteenth-century, fostered a transplanted community of East Coast immigrants.

This influx of Easterners brought money and enterprise to Marshall. Most of

Left: **These pineapple-shaped finials, inspired by the homeowner's fond memories of Hawaii, were also a symbol of hospitality.**

Right: **The Honolulu House, built in 1860 at a cost of approximately fifteen thousand dollars, was designed to emulate a similar home occupied by the owner while he served as the United States Consul to the Sandwich Islands. Upon his death the home was publicly auctioned with all of its contents, "including Furniture, Books, Paintings, Engravings, Sea Shells and Curiosities."**

the new arrivals were young, well educated, and ambitious. Most families were eager to acquire land, not only for their own home-sites but also as real estate investments. These speculators, financed by their wealthy New England relatives, purchased vast tracts of land on the outskirts of Marshall.

Other entrepreneurs capitalized on Marshall's convenient location next to the Kalamazoo River by erecting water-driven gristmills. George Ketchum had opened a sawmill by the summer of 1831 to supply lumber to the craftsmen who were busily building structures for the growing local population. By winter the residents of Marshall had constructed a schoolhouse, general store, hotel, workshops, and a simple log cabin for each resettled family.

These wilderness dwellings were rudimentary compared to the prestigious estates the settlers had known in New England. Framed cottages replaced log cabins the next season. To recapture their previously elegant lifestyle, relocated Eastern families, financed by bank loans, personal assets, and speculative deals, began building stately residences that dwarfed the earlier cottages and cabins.

With this pronounced architectural style came greater cultural expectations from the community. Teachers and ministers were commissioned by the town leaders to guide the minds and souls of Marshall. One of the first local settlers, Reverend Pierce, established his personal residence as a "house of hospitality" that often served as a meeting place for important discussions.

A lawyer named Isaac Crary frequented these meetings, and Pierce and Crary were instrumental in planning the future of Marshall. Together they devised a master plan for the territorial public school system. Besides promoting education, the leaders of Marshall encouraged religious participation; various denominations met in homes, schools and the public courthouse. In early Marshall the separation of church and state was an impractical distinction.

By 1837 Michigan had gained statehood, and Marshall blossomed into an active township of over a thousand people. As the town grew it also diversified, and the community included two bakeries, three churches matched by three taverns, four blacksmiths, five grocery stores, six dry goods' shops, and at least a dozen doctors and lawyers. Businesses also included pharmacies, jewelers, tailors, milliners, shoemakers, coopers, wagon and carriage builders, painters, carpenters, and stonecutters.

As Marshall entered the 1840s prolific construction of brick and stone buildings gave the town a prestigious appearance; local politicians began to promote Marshall for the "state seat of government." With its centralized location in the state, Marshall was preferred by American businesses as a trade center over Detroit, which had been economically challenged by the British across the Detroit River. The constituents of Michigan saw Marshall, with its refined culture, prosperous economy, and distinguished architecture, as a more appropriate state capital location.

For the next decade optimism soared in Marshall. Unofficial state maps identified it as the new capital, and land speculators drove real estate prices to inflationary levels. Senator James Gordon formally proposed Marshall's selection before the State Congress, but Detroit politicians resisted. In a devastating compromise, Michigan's legislators arbitrarily chose the obscure central village of Lansing for the new state capital.

Marshall's political bubble burst, and the town's economic status, which had been throttled for years by speculative investment, temporarily collapsed. Financial revival came in the 1850s from the Michigan Central Railroad, which brought increased commerce with its passengers, employees, and freight. Again, Marshall's central location on a main transportation route made it an attractive place for people to stop and spend their money.

In the days before railroad dining cars, Marshall became known to regular train travelers as "the chicken pie stop." Passengers frequented convenient restaurants and taverns near the station while railroad engines were serviced for the next leg of their journey. Train mechanics and crews were stationed in Marshall to maintain the railroad machine shops, which added to the labor force and increased the demand for employee housing.

The 1860s were boom years for Marshall despite the uncertainty caused by the specter of civil war. Newspapers proudly extolled the importance of Marshall as a link "in the great chain of railroads" that would soon stretch from the Atlantic to the Pacific coast. War shipments combined with heavy travel to the Western frontier boosted the profits of the Michigan Central Railroad, which fortified its lighter "T-rails" with heavy gauge iron rails.

As settlers from the East Coast swarmed through Marshall, they brought along new pattern books for house-building with novel

This formal Italian Villa house, built in 1869, maintains the classic floor plan of a central entry-way with formal parlors on each side. One of the owners of this home was William Wallace Cook, a well-known author of boys' books, who wrote a story a week from this residence over a period of three decades. This neighborhood is reached by what was once known as the Old Plank Road, a toll highway that was lined with wooden planks to keep carriages from slipping in the mud.

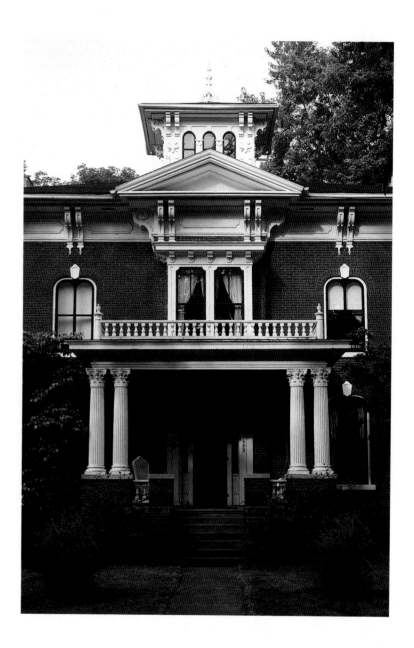

As the Victorian age evolved men and women assumed stereotypical roles. Husbands commuted to the work place as businessmen and laborers while their wives remained at home as isolated and unpaid housewives. After the working man challenged the daily rigors of the marketplace he returned home at night to the domestic tranquility of his wife and their Victorian home. The expectations of men's and women's roles were further reinforced by the social, cultural and economic forces of industrialization.

By the 1850s Marshall was conveniently linked by railroads to both Detroit and Chicago. It became popular and affordable for business travelers to commute into larger cities from their home towns. One such Michigan business trip was humorously chronicled by a Marshall newspaper to illustrate a day in the life of a Victorian commuter:

"Go-In Lemons, a wide-awake business man, who loves to snuff the morning air, can leave Marshall at 2 AM, take a cup of coffee in Detroit, go to the Peninsula Bank, purchase a check, 'take the cars' at 7 AM, return to Marshall by 11 AM, meet and kiss his wife at the Depot, eat a chicken pie at 'Major Banks', chat with his business acquaintances, take the lightning train and arrive at Detroit at 2 PM, go immediately to a barber shop and bath house, dine sumptuously at the Biddle House, call on the Detroit editors, stir them up, take a delicious and fragrant cup of tea, served up in excellent style at the Michigan Exchange, stroll over to Johnson's Hotel, smoke a glorious Havana, hop on the night train at 6 PM, arrive in Marshall at 11 PM, and find his wife waiting for him at home with an ice lemonade, a roll of hot muffins, and a bowl of sweet milk and delicious berries, go to bed, and dream of Heaven. There, Mother, we've said it all."

Orson Fowler, the first proponent of the "octagonal mode of building," lectured at Marshall in 1850. This unique building was the only one of its kind in town, and its unorthodox design and geometrical construction drew much attention in 1856.

designs and methods for construction. These influences proliferated quickly around town, and previously plain cottages sported fancy bargeboard details in their gables. Gothic Revival and Italianate architectural styles were popular during the postwar housing boom that propelled Marshall into a construction frenzy.

But as Marshall home-builders myopically focused their efforts on house construction, the presumption that the railroad was less important to the economy caused a lack of local support for civic assistance to the Michigan Central Railroad. With decreased maintenance funds and financial support from Marshall, the railroad relocated its shops and yards twenty-five miles east to Jackson. Unwittingly, Marshall created an economic recession by ignoring the railroad, and as the trains bypassed Marshall, so did progress.

When the Michigan Central Railroad departed Marshall in 1874, the town fell into a fifty-year slumber. Without the prospect for economic growth, real estate speculators and venture capitalists abandoned Marshall for frontier towns in the West. New construction ceased, and residential renovation became financially unattractive as the town's population began to dwindle.

In frustration, residents shifted their attention from real estate to cottage industries. Although fewer people lived in

ADAM CROSSWHITE

In a northern Michigan town of resettled Easterners, the story of Adam Crosswhite exemplifies the distinguished character and moral fiber of Marshall's citizens during the controversial era of slavery. Adam Crosswhite, the son of a slave and her white master, was born in Kentucky and given to his white half-sister as a servant at an early age. During his adult bondage Crosswhite married a slave, and together they had four children. As his offspring matured, Adam feared that they would be sold and his family separated. In a daring escape across the Ohio River, the Crosswhites fled to Indiana; there the Quakers and "underground railroad" helped the family to resettle in Marshall, where they lived peacefully and raised a fifth child.

Adam, however, feared reprisal from his former master. His fears were confirmed in 1846, when Francis Troutman, grandson of Adam's owner in Kentucky, and two accomplices attempted to reclaim the Crosswhites. Troutman intended to have the Crosswhites arrested under the Fugitive Slave Law and extradite them to Kentucky. When Troutman approached the Crosswhite cabin, Adam and his wife refused to admit them or surrender. While Troutman attempted a forcible entry, a crowd of Marshall citizens arrived. Troutman said he would make no claim for the freeborn youngest child, since his only concern was in taking the rest of the family back to Kentucky.

Troutman's words enraged the Crosswhites' friends and neighbors. More townspeople arrived and questioned Troutman about the moral justification of forcibly removing any of Marshall's citizens, black or white. Troutman demanded the arrest of the Crosswhite family, but the local sheriff reversed his prior sympathies and decided instead to arrest Troutman and his thugs on charges of "assault, battery, and housebreaking." As they stood trial the next day, secret plans were made to get the Crosswhites into Canada. The family sought refuge from anti-slavery sympathizers, who quickly escorted the family to Detroit, where they escaped across the Canadian border to freedom.

The plans for this home built in 1870 were drawn by a well-known Marshall carpenter, whom the local newspaper "suspected of possessing architectural talent — he has made a very handsome house on paper for Mr. Hulett."

The cupolas on top of Italian Villa homes allowed for natural light to help illuminate upstairs rooms, which lacked electrical lights until the latter part of the Victorian Era.

Right: **The original owner of this home, built in 1868, was an engineer and a builder. A spacious kitchen was added to the residence before the turn of the century by its second owner, granddaughter to one of the town's pioneer families.**

MARSHALL, *The Crossroads of Progress*

Marshall, those citizens who chose to stay began to market their knowledge and ingenuity beyond the city limits. With the arrival of mail order advertising, Marshall became a home office for health products that were promoted to a national clientele.

Patent medicines of all kinds were sold and distributed through the Marshall Post Office. Remedies, cures, devices, and gimmicks of endless variety were offered to a naive consumer market. Devices of dubious distinction such as the Marshall Folding Bathtub and "Pink Pills for Pale People" were sold to gullible long-distance dilettantes. Curiously, the prosperity of the town's financial success was revitalized by the health claims of its charlatans.

Marshall exercised its reborn civic health, as it always had, through new architectural expression. The local snake oil barons and magic-elixir elite decorated the town with fanciful Queen Anne Victorians that reflected their pretentious livelihood. But this capricious display of temporary success did not prevent the malaise that recaptured Marshall at the end of the 1800s.

Marshall's panacea for financial disease suffered a crippling relapse when the federal government passed the Pure Food and Drug Act in 1900. This law forbade the distribution for sale without prior government analysis, testing, and approval of any ingestible substance that promised medical

Left: **This Italian Villa home, known as Oakhill, was built in 1858 and remained with the Brewer family for over one hundred years. Many of the original furnishings still remain in the house. Outbuildings on the property include a carriage house, garage, smoke shed, pig barn and corn crib. The original carriage steps and hitching post are still in place.**

Right: **Oakhill** *epitomizes the quality of historical architecture in Marshall. During its construction all the bricks were made by local craftsmen at the site.*

benefits. Of course most of the potions, powders, and pills that had been advertised as miracle cures could not survive the scrutiny of the federal Food and Drug Administration, and Marshall's medicine merchants went out of business.

One Marshall businessman who did prevail over government interference was Harold C. Brooks, the owner of the Brooks Rupture Appliance Company, a mail order business that marketed trusses for hernia problems. In the early 1900s he used the profits from his business to purchase at least a dozen important buildings in Marshall which he maintained until suitable families could invest and renovate these historic homes. Brooks was very popular with local citizens, and in 1925 they elected him Mayor of Marshall.

Brooks' visionary campaign to restore the architectural heritage of Marshall started long before it became fashionable to save Victorians. For over sixty years he continued his preservation efforts by using much of his personal wealth to rescue abandoned buildings. His exemplary actions inspired many families to return to Marshall and recapture its former elegance and glory.

As a result, many homeowners and restorers, who came to town after Marshall's decades of obscure isolation, were new-comers seeking to rediscover a small-town atmosphere with traditional American

values. They cherished the rows of vintage Victorians within walking distance of downtown, the stately old trees that lined its streets, and the peaceful parks and fountains where families could gather to enjoy picnics and share quiet conversations.

Today the railroad bypasses Marshall — there is no trace of the trains, tracks, and taverns that popularized this town during the previous century. But people have not forgotten its historical significance. Since 1963, the Marshall Historical Society has organized an annual autumn Historic Home Tour. Victorian enthusiasts return each year to commemorate Marshall's majesty on the "Crossroads of Progress."

This sunburst pattern, with its many variations, appears in several different locations on this home. Transom-framed stained glass windows were popular in Queen Anne architecture, because they supplied ambient light over entrance doors.

Left: **This Queen Anne home, constructed on a corner lot in 1887, was built at a cost of about six thousand dollars. The elaborate interior plan created much favorable comment in the local papers: "To the left is a door leading from the vestibule into the double parlors. They are pleasant in the extreme and present a view of both streets that cannot be improved."**

This Italianate building, built for Liberty Engine Number One in 1851, is Illinois' oldest firehouse, and its cupola still holds a working fire bell. The firehouse was built of brick, as were many houses and commercial buildings in town, because of frequent fires.

GALENA

Riverfront Fortune

"Galena" is the Latin word for lead ore. It is also the name of a small town in Illinois that became America's primary source for lead ore in the nineteenth-century. Located near the east bank of the Mississippi River, Galena prospered as a riverfront trade center for the region's lucrative mining activities, when steamboats provided convenient and economical transportation for shipping its valuable ore to port cities downstream.

The topography surrounding Galena for approximately thirty miles in all directions is identified by geologists as "driftless" because glaciers never eroded its mineral-rich upper layers. American Indian tribes dwelled in this river region for centuries before the arrival of white settlers, and the fertile land and ample water supply provided ideal growing conditions for their crops. The Indians also excavated small caves to extract lead for use in their hand-

Right: **Heritage and hospitality are the trademarks of this historically rich town. As Victorian architect Andrew Jackson Downing wrote, "When smiling lawns and tasteful cottages begin to embellish a country, we know that order and culture are established."**

forged tools and hunting weapons.

In the 1700s French explorers traveled up the Mississippi River to investigate the opportunities for settlement and commerce. A Frenchman named Lasuer encountered the Indian settlements and described the present day location of Galena as, "on a small river that entered the 'Great River' in its east bank." Trappers and traders identified this confluence as the mouth of the Fever River where it turbulently mixed waters with the Mississippi.

After the Louisiana Purchase of 1803 Galena's growing reputation for concentrated deposits of lead ore began to attract hopeful prospectors. Steamboats began to explore the upper Mississippi River, which brought passengers and cargo from riverfront towns in the South. Other settlers came from the East by following tributary rivers that flowed into the mighty Mississippi where they could board steamers heading upriver.

The first steamboat to ascend the Fever River carried Dr. Moses Meeker and Daniel Smith Harris, who had traveled from Ohio in search of opportunity along the Mississippi River for their families and friends. Several years later, in 1824, Dr. Meeker, the Harris family, and about thirty other settlers left their Cincinnati homes destined for Galena on a keelboat loaded with eighty tons of mining equipment and provisions. They safely floated down the calm Ohio River to meet the powerful Mississippi, where the challenging part of their river journey began.

The rapid and high waters of the Mississippi made it impossible to paddle or pole their way upstream, so the crew resorted to various towing techniques to pull their keelboat upriver towards Galena. By running the boat close to shore, the men on board "bushwacked" their way up the river by pulling on overhanging bushes and trees. Another tactic, called "warping," was to send a long rope ahead in a skiff; after the rope was secured to a tree, the crew members would pull their boat up towards it.

After a slow and arduous trip up the Mississippi River, the Meeker and Harris party arrived in Galena to find about one hundred white miners and approximately one hundred and fifty Indians digging into the hillsides for lead. The new arrivals continued to live on their boat until temporary log shelters could be built. In 1825, Dr. Meeker discovered new lead mines in an area called "West Diggings" that proved to be the richest ore strike in the Galena area.

By 1826 town lots were laid out, as the local population grew to a mixture of about four hundred miners, traders, and Indians, who coexisted tenuously in tents, crude shacks, and log cabins. When claims and

This was the home built in 1855 by one of Galena's earliest settlers and most prominent steamboat pilots, Captain Daniel Harris. This Andrew Jackson Downing design is published in his 1850 book The Architecture of Country Houses. Downing describes the home as one suitable for "the country life of those who live in the Middle United States." The second floor oriel window is meant to "court the sunshine." According to Downing, "the cost of this house, finished in a simple and appropriate manner, would be between six and seven thousand dollars."

GALENA, *Riverfront Fortune* 135

disputes over mining stakes caused confusion and squabbles, an "official" newspaper began to publish the names and locations of registered miners and their strikes. This information was conspicuously displayed in the new post office, which became the first postal facility in northern Illinois.

Animosity between the native Indians and white immigrant settlers intensified during the rest of the decade. In 1830 the Winnebago tribe led an uprising against the town of Galena, which was followed by the Black Hawk War in 1832. These hostilities brought intercession by federal troops who instituted martial law and established a military camp in town.

United States soldiers built and garrisoned a fortified block house, and a secret passage linked their military camp to an underground refuge hidden under an inconspicuous log house. The Indians were deterred from further attacks by the military presence in Galena, although they continued to survey the town from an elevation called Horse Shoe Mound. Chief Black Hawk, fearing reprisal from the resentful residents of Galena, eventually retreated to Council Hill to conduct treaty negotiations with the federal government.

During the latter 1830s, Galena developed into a gateway trading center for the mining boom that overtook the area. The Fever River was renamed the Galena

Left: From this belvedere, Nelson Stillman could look across Galena to Stillman's Dry Goods Store, which not only supplied his pantry but also profitably furnished his home with magnificent and opulent works of art. In spite of their wealth, the Stillman's were concerned with the community and the future of its children as he is credited to having started one of the first public schools in Galena.

Right: Galena merchant Nelson Stillman built this home in 1858 on the edge of his large estate just outside the city limits. He arrived in Galena around 1837 and operated a successful dry goods' store. The home is considered to be one of the finest built in Galena. It is located across the road from General Grant's local residence, and the families frequently dined together in the Stillman home.

River to improve the town's image. A second wave of fortune seekers began mining the north side of the river in an area that was called the "new diggings" to distinguish it from the original lead mines. Wholesalers, entrepreneurs, and speculators bought, sold, and traded various commodities for distribution to markets up and down the Mississippi River.

The daughter of one Galena businessman described the enterprising town this way: "There were great wharves crowded with millions of dollars worth of lead ore. The waterfront was lined up and down with wholesale stores that distributed their goods to the far Northwest, including stores for forts and Indian trade goods. Here were gathered all kinds of people — speculators from the East, men from still further west, which was a virtual wilderness, in buckskin clothes, miners, Indians, so many French from St. Louis; such a promiscuous crowd, climbing the hills, jostling one another in the narrow streets, only two principal streets, really, Main and Bench, one above the other, then side streets running up the ravines. What a town! A veritable metropolis."

Galena gained notoriety for being the wildest and largest settlement town in the Illinois Territory. A local Temperance Society was formed in 1838 to battle the public drunkenness that proliferated in the town's various saloons, "groceries" (taverns),

and hotels. By 1839 Galena had increased in size to ten thousand residents, many of who began building attractive homes on the hillsides overlooking the commercial district along the river.

During the 1840s Galena became the most important commercial center along the Mississippi River north of St. Louis. Shrewd traders and wholesalers in Galena monopolized the distribution of consumer goods to the territories of Iowa, Wisconsin, and Minnesota. Settlers in the Northern wilderness depended on the steamships of the Mississippi for survival, and most of these riverboats were owned and operated by Galena businessmen.

By 1845 the steam tonnage on Western rivers in the United States rivaled the cargo transported by the entire British merchant fleet. More steamboats were traveling between Galena and St. Louis than all the other traffic flowing along the Mississippi and Ohio rivers combined. Since no port town was closer to the lead mines and smelters than Galena, over eighty percent of the nation's lead ore during the 1840s was exported from Galena's wharves to metal markets around the world.

Every steamship stopped in Galena for passengers and provisions when it cruised the upper Mississippi River. The town levee was widened and lengthened to accommodate up to eighteen ships simultaneously.

Many of the earlier steamboats were owned and operated by their captains. As these ships grew in size and operating expense, the majority of riverboats were sold to their suppliers in Galena. These suppliers used the advantages of exclusive ownership to control and manipulate the river transportation trade.

By 1850 wholesale and retail businesses in Galena were thriving, and lead ore production was only one aspect of the town's diversified economy. Steamboat ownership proved to be as profitable for local entrepreneurs as the mining business, and huge profits were reinvested into commercial developments and elegant mansions. Towards the end of the decade, lead production decreased, but Galena's economy continued to prosper with the influx of immigrants who raised the town's population to an all-time high of fourteen thousand in 1858.

What Galena's millionaires failed to recognize, however, was the impact that the railroads would have on their steamboat enterprises. When the Illinois Central Railroad reached Galena and the Mississippi

Ornamental wrought-iron fences bordered the boundary between city lots to distinguish urban properties, but ornamental fences were seldom needed to surround country houses.

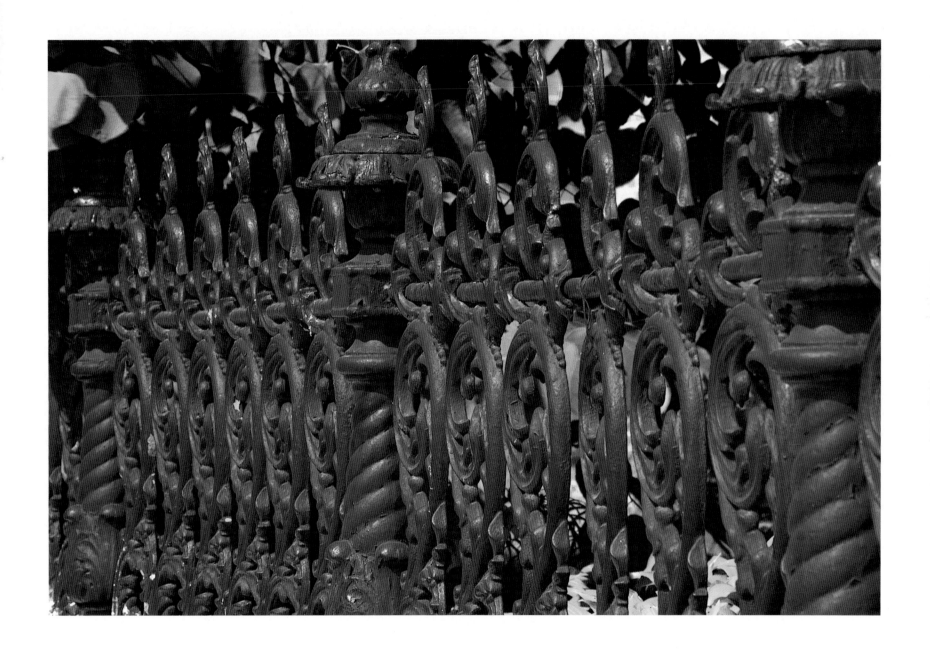

GALENA, *Riverfront Fortune*

River in the late 1850s, riverboat owners believed that it would bring more business to their shipping trade. They perceived the railroads as a cooperative link to expanded trade and commerce, but the highly competitive railroad owners relentlessly fought to replace the trade routes along the riverways.

The railroads wasted no time in laying tracks parallel to the Missouri, Ohio, and Mississippi Rivers. To lure business away from the steamboat companies, railroad promoters offered temporarily discounted freight deals to independent distributors and wholesalers. This tactic undercut river trade during the navigable seasons. When the riverboat season ended, the railroads doubled or tripled their cargo rates. Galena became a center of controversy as steamboat and train operators competed for control of commercial trade along the Mississippi River.

As competition intensified, steamboat companies began to undermine each other by relying on cutthroat trading policies, unrealistic wharfage rates at river landings, and inadequate terminal facilities for holding cargo. Access to shallow-water ports such as Galena became difficult due to the silt accumulation in the Galena River. Clear-cutting of forests along the river, combined with strip-mining near the river banks, caused severe erosion, which filled the Galena levee and steamship channel with mud.

SHOWBOATS

Showboats were floating theaters that cruised the inland waterways of the Midwest to give shoreside performances at various settlements along the river banks. These drifting performers provided the isolated pioneers of the American frontier with welcome entertainment. The remote riverfront towns along the Mississippi, Missouri, and Ohio Rivers were treated to a diverse blend of serious, comical, and musical entertainment.

Beginning with small rafts that merely drifted downstream and carried a few musicians, showboating progressed to a sensational level that featured custom-built entertainment palaces with hundreds of costumed cast members. The first large commercial craft was a one hundred foot barge with a covered superstructure that housed a stage illuminated by candle footlights, a musician's pit, and wooden benches to seat an audience of about two hundred. Inspired by the financial success of this showboat, dozens of floating acts navigated the Midwestern rivers in the 1840s and 1850s.

Program material ranged from vaudeville to Shakespeare, minstrel shows to opera, circus acts to political debates. Almost anything that could be put on a portable stage found its way to the showboat circuit. Most frontier audiences were understandably starved for entertainment, and promoters sometimes used their boats to feature dubious talent who either performed material beyond their capabilities or abused artistic license.

Eventually showboats gained a tawdry reputation as floating dens of iniquity, where gamblers, bartenders, and charlatans vied for the customer's money. An exception to this trend was provided by several legitimate circus boats. The most spectacular was the Floating Circus Palace, which measured one hundred feet long and thirty-five feet wide; the amphibious amphitheater seated thirty-four hundred in its dress circle and two galleries. This steam-powered one-ring circus carried over one hundred performers, trainers, staff, crew and animals.

When the distinctive steam calliope heralded the imminent arrival of a showboat, river residents for miles along the shore would eagerly race to meet the performers and purchase tickets for the evening show. As time went on, rival showboats became even more luxurious, featuring private loges, central heating, and elegant accouterments. Until the railroads stole their audiences by bringing novel forms of entertainment to the Western frontier, the showboat made a popular contribution to American culture.

Steam Calliope's announced the arrival of Mississippi showboats, which would perform at the landings of riverfront communities; circuses, dramatic productions and musical extravaganzas all delivered stage entertainment aboard paddlewheelers.

Dredging efforts proved temporary and ineffective, so wholesalers and traders in Galena were compelled to abandon their steamships and depend on the railroads to export their commodities. To further depress the local economy, the output of lead from the district declined dramatically; the richer local ore deposits were exhausted, while lead mines in Missouri increased in productivity. Galena businessmen, who for decades had thrived on a readily available supply of lead ore, combined with a steady demand for their steamship transportation, suffered a financial decline in both supply and demand.

During the 1860s Galena's economy continued to deteriorate. The Civil War brought the blockade of the Mississippi River and the interruption of railroad freight service, disrupting both of Galena's traditional trading links to port towns situated north and south along the river. Wholesale trading became impossible, and many businesses in Galena were forced to close. During the following decade the assessed valuation for the city plummeted by over seventy-five percent, and municipal bond holders were forced to take one quarter for each dollar invested.

After the war the railroads continued to expand westward, which popularized train travel along east-west routes between cities like Chicago and the Western frontier.

Left: **Inspired by the recent "colorist" movement, the owners of this Victorian selected an autumn palette to repaint their previously white home. Lifelong Galena neighbors commented immediately on details that went unnoticed until this house was painted in a polychromatic palette.**

Right: **Built in 1892, this was the home of William Ridd who achieved affluence after he married the daughter of his boss at the Galena Lumber Sash and Door, where he formed a partnership with his father-in-law.**

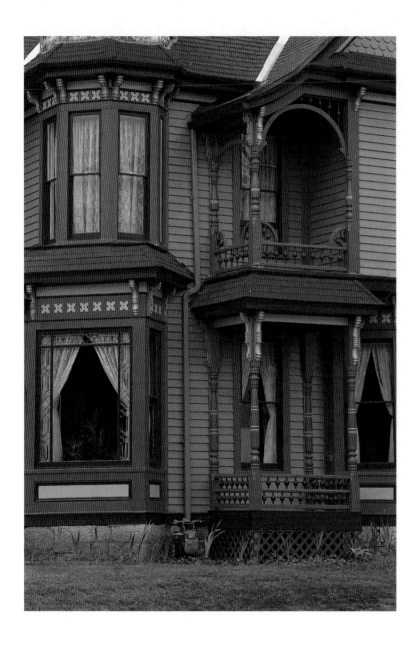

Galena, on the other hand, had traditionally relied on commercial traffic that flowed along the north-south direction of the Mississippi River. With the South economically crippled from the war, Galena lost its previous Southern market contacts and transportation routes, while the railroads had Galena's access to the Northwest.

Ironically, the Civil War, which robbed Galena of its prosperity, also gave it a hero. Ulysses S. Grant, who had moved his family to Galena in 1860, worked his way up through the volunteer ranks to become a highly decorated Union general in the war. When he returned to Galena in 1865, the national limelight shined on the town's most famous citizen, who was elected President of the United States in 1868. After Grant's time in the White House, he returned to Galena for over a decade, where he enjoyed the hospitality and tranquillity of his adopted home town.

Not even Grant's popularity, however, could save Galena from its isolation in the late 1800s. Republicans and Democrats blamed each other for the demise of their town, and the local government became polarized and divided as a result. Lacking unified civic leadership, Galena faltered in the absence of political and economic direction, and local businesses and their owners left town for opportunities in the West. The town's

144

Left: **The Belevedere *stands as a symbol to the early success of J.R. Jones who arrived as a young man in Galena in 1840 and advanced from a nominally salaried clerk to full partnership in a supply firm. Jones was later appointed as a U.S. Marshall and became a trusted friend of Abraham Lincoln's.***

Right: **Built in 1857, the Belvedere *was named for the "beautiful view" from the cupola structure sitting on top of this home. It now contains furnishings purchased from Liberace's estate as well as draperies and art used in the movie* Gone With the Wind. *The dining room features an original Tiffany chandelier — it was acquired at the cost of purchasing the building that originally housed this unique fixture!***

Once the only source of fresh water in the home, this traditional hand pump serves as a vintage reminder a convenience taken for granted by Victorian enthusiasts today.

ULYSSES S. GRANT

Ulysses S. Grant, his wife, and their four children moved from St. Louis to become Galena residents in 1860 after his army service in the Mexican War. Grant worked in his father's leather store where he earned a modest salary. On April 12, 1861, when news of the attack on Fort Sumter by Confederates came to Galena over the telegraph wires, every soldier and Republican in northern Illinois prepared to fight in defense of the Union.

Three days later, when Confederate soldiers captured the fort, President Lincoln issued a Proclamation of War which called for the immediate recruitment of seventy-five thousand Union soldiers. A town meeting was hastily called in Galena with Captain Grant presiding as chairman. The majority in attendance endorsed the President's statement, and many of the younger men volunteered for military service in the Union Army.

Grant was appointed by the Governor of Illinois to command an inexperienced local volunteer regiment. The skillful captain carefully disciplined his troops for battle, and in the ensuing months he led them to numerous victories in combat. By September of 1861 Grant had already risen to the rank of Brigadier General for all Union volunteers.

As Commanding General during the critical months of the Civil War Grant led his loyal Union soldiers to capture several key Confederate forts and towns. General Grant ultimately pursued and surrounded Robert E. Lee's army, forcing the Commanding General of the Confederate Army to surrender his rebel forces in April of 1865 at the Appomattox Court House. Grant offered Lee magnanimous terms of surrender that avoided humiliating treason trials.

Following the war, General Grant returned to Galena in August of 1865. The townspeople received their war hero with unbounded patriotism, and admirers came from across the nation to congratulate him. Flags and banners decorated every street corner in Galena, and an immense arch spanned the main street, bearing the inscription: "Hail to the Chief who in triumph advances!"

The symbol of Union victory, U.S. Grant, was the logical Republican candidate for president in 1868. The American voters readily elected Grant as their chief executive, hoping that his strong leadership would eliminate the corruption that had crept into Washington since Lincoln's assassination. Grant, however, perceived his presidential role as a federal administrator because he felt that congressional actions better represented the political will of the people.

Grant presumptuously ran his administration like an army headquarters, which led to scandals such as "Black Friday," "Credit Mobilier," and the "Salary Grab." A man of scrupulous honesty, Grant naively accepted presents from admirers and associated with nefarious speculators such as Jay Gould and James Fisk. Grant belatedly realized that his connections with corrupt financiers were politically imprudent; his damaged reputation ultimately prevented his election to another presidential term.

Grant's administration had temporarily ended inflation, curtailed the Federal Debt, and established the first Civil Service Commission, but the stress of war and political life had exhausted the leader from Illinois. Grant wearily returned with his family to Galena where he was content to recuperate from his eventful career in relative tranquillity. The Grants left Galena for the last time in 1881 to reside in New York City. They donated their home as a museum, complete with souvenirs, pictures, and artifacts from the Civil War and White House eras as a parting gift to the citizens of Galena.

*Left: **This house was built in 1876 on six hundred acres of farmland as the home of James M. Ryan, one Galena's most respected citizens. After moving to the area in 1846, Ryan soon established a wholesale and retail grocery partnership with his brother, William. He became sole owner of the retail grocery when William relocated to Dubuque to start a pork-packing business. James soon followed his brother's venture into the butcher business, and eventually the brothers successfully dominated the meat-packing industry for the entire region, second only to Chicago.***

*Right: **An urn-shaped vase is the focal point of this classic Renaissance-style stained glass window featured in the foyer of a Galena Victorian.***

population and revenues fell dramatically, and Galena became a forgotten boom town of the nineteenth-century.

Most of Galena's beautiful Victorian buildings were abandoned and allowed to deteriorate for decades. Following World War II, historical interest in Galena became popular, and town leaders established a historic preservation ordinance in 1951 to prevent the demolition of significant vintage structures. Descendants of original homeowners and Victorian enthusiasts returned to Galena to renovate traditional homes and mansions.

These days Galena is again a popular destination that caters mostly to weekend and summer visitors from Chicago. Guided town tours on open-air trolleys, theme festivals and cultural events, and public admission to many of Galena's elegant mansions provides the historical enthusiast with vivid impressions of its colorful heritage. From the economic glory of its past to the historical treasures it offers today, Galena continues to be a "Riverfront Fortune."

Dubuque grew dramatically in economic importance through its strategic utilization of both railroads and riverboat transportation. The introduction of the mechanical reaper to Midwestern farmers assured commercial prosperity and Dubuque became the transportation hub for the traders in Iowa. This bustling port community experienced rapid growth in the mid 1850s, as three thousand emigrants a month arrived in Iowa, and many of these settlers made Dubuque their new home.

DUBUQUE

Victorian Variety

THE VICTORIAN EXPRESS

DUBUQUE
IOWA

ALL ABOARD EXCURSION

CAR	TICKET NO.	RES. NO.
	007	288
TRAIN NO.	FIRST CLASS	
91		

PASSENGER RECEIPT

DESTINATION

Dubuque, Iowa is a Midwestern blend of cultural and architectural traditions. During the last two centuries a diversity of ethnic groups has influenced the growth and development of this waterfront community. Located on the west bank of the upper Mississippi River, Dubuque exhibits representative examples for all major styles of Victorian architecture.

Because of its accessible location Dubuque attracted European immigrants of various nationalities during its settlement. Natives of France, Spain, England, Scotland, Ireland, and Germany all came to the Iowa Territory in search of land and opportunity. Each wave of foreign newcomers established its own identity in Dubuque by building distinctive neighborhoods that evoked its cultural background.

For over two hundred years, Dubuque has manifested the chronological evolution of architecture in America. The original rustic cabins of French trappers and miners along the river were replaced during the nineteenth-century by Victorian homes in the Italianate, Gothic, Second Empire, Queen Anne, and Stick styles. As architects introduced new forms of construction to the American home builder, local interpretations of national building trends emerged in provincial towns like Dubuque.

Louis Joliet and Father Marquette first explored the Upper Mississippi Valley in 1673 for the French government. Nicholas Perrot returned in 1690 to the area near the eventual site of Dubuque where he taught the local Miami Indian tribes how to mine for lead ore. Indians and Frenchmen helped each other hunt and mine in the river region for the next hundred years.

In 1788, the cooperative Indian leaders granted a French trapper and miner named Julien Dubuque permission to establish a permanent site along the Mississippi River, which became known as "Dubuque." Several years later, Baron Carondolet, governor of Upper Louisiana, granted Monsieur Dubuque the first and largest of three Spanish Land Grants in the region. The so-called "Mines of Spain" comprised a nine-mile tract adjoining the Mississippi River between the Little Maquoketa and Tete de Mont Creeks.

For the next two decades, Dubuque utilized his settlement primarily as a trading and mining outpost. Before each winter arrived, Dubuque departed Iowa with a boatload of furs and lead for St. Louis, where he traded his goods for provisions and materials to operate the mines during the next season. Following the Louisiana Purchase in 1803 President Jefferson sent Lieutenant Zebulon Pike on a scouting mission up the Mississippi River; Pike stopped and conferred with Dubuque before continuing upstream to explore the extent of the United States' newly-acquired Louisiana Territory.

Dubuque's mining efforts were generally unprofitable, and soon he fell heavily into debt to a trader named August Chouteau. To cover his losses Dubuque gave the southern half of his Spanish Land Grant to Chouteau. When Dubuque died in 1810, the Chouteau family attempted to take control of the "Mines of Spain," but they were repelled by the Sauk and Fox Indians

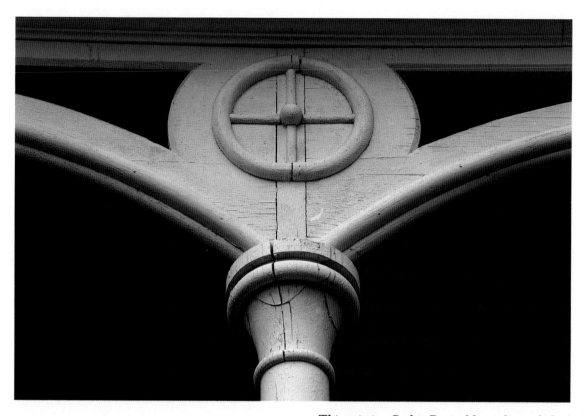

This pristine Gothic Revival home has only had four owners over the past one hundred years. It was originally the home of a local businessman who owned a thriving stationery, book, and wallpaper store around the turn of the century.

Left: **Nestled in its wooded bluffside setting, with all the features country cottages were meant to possess, is the most significant remaining Gothic Revival home in Dubuque. This home was built in 1890, ten years after this style went out of fashion. Nevertheless, the builder dauntlessly followed a design that first became popular in pattern books circulated during the 1850s.**

who claimed that Dubuque had never owned the mines. The Indians insisted that Dubuque was only given access to their land, and their legal right to land ownership was eventually upheld in the United States Supreme Court.

Following the Black Hawk War Treaty in 1833, white settlers returned to Dubuque and established it as a commercial trading center for the increasing steamboat traffic along the Mississippi River. As more people arrived on the paddlewheelers from New Orleans and St. Louis, Dubuque grew into a flourishing town; it incorporated itself in 1837, and four years later an official city charter was adopted. During the 1840s, Dubuque prospered as the hub of tri-state commerce for Iowa, Illinois, and Wisconsin.

Since Dubuque attracted immigrants from a wide range of countries, ethnic neighborhoods emerged that housed concentrations of residents from similar origins. The settlers that first came to Dubuque after the French trappers and miners were mostly Irish and German descendants, and they generally remained in segregated residential blocks near the riverfront. Although these different groups did not typically socialize with each other due to language and cultural barriers, they were gradually integrated by the economic and political environment that they shared in Dubuque.

Although lead mining slowly decreased in the area, agriculture, grain mills, and the lumber industry thrived around Dubuque. By patronizing both the riverboat and railroad transportation companies Dubuque's wholesalers and traders held a competitive advantage over other cities in the region, cities that depended exclusively on land or water routes to distribute their products. Shippers used steamboats to carry their exports downriver to seaport cities such as New Orleans, while railroads enabled Dubuque to supply Eastern factories with raw materials in exchange for finished goods.

Transportation also stimulated local manufacturing. Augustin A. Cooper came to Dubuque in 1846 to establish his own wagon-making business. Cooper marketed the "Old Reliable" wagon, which was sold throughout the United States and was popularized by thousands of Mormons migrating to Utah. The Cooper Wagon Plant eventually covered an entire city block, and twenty-five acres of riverfront property were devoted to drying Iowa lumber for use in the construction of Cooper's wooden wagons and buggies.

As the local economy expanded, real estate investment and development also intensified; civic leaders encouraged the construction of magnificent public and private buildings. During the early 1850s,

Left: **One of Dubuque's most prolific architects, Fridolin J. Heer, immigrated from Germany to Illinois before moving to Dubuque in 1868. He worked as a master stonecutter before turning to architecture in 1870, where he maintained his position as a leading architect until his death in 1910. His son joined the firm in 1887 after studying at the School of Architecture in Stuttgart, Germany and continued the family business until 1934. The firm's many designs included some of the most important landmarks ever constructed in Dubuque, including the County Court House.**

Right: **Built in 1873 as a final monument to Second Empire architecture by noted architect Fridolin Heer, the clock tower is built with heavy stone caps, lintels, and is three stories high. The clock was operated by means of weights running up and down a shaft. This mechanism was wound daily by two boys who spent an hour-and-a-half at the task, until a motor was installed to wind the clock in 1900.**

Dubuque experienced a flurry of urban architectural growth. Elaborate churches featuring stained glass windows from Louis Tiffany Studios in New York were erected, and huge warehouse facilities were built along the bustling waterfront in anticipation of increased commercial trade.

Just as national prosperity had blessed Dubuque's economy with good fortune, the financial panic that plagued the country in 1857 brought local depression to Dubuque's businesses. Many building projects were suspended for several years, while Dubuque struggled to recover from the recession brought on by the consequences of overspeculation and unregulated banking. To exacerbate the situation, The Panic of 1857 was followed by a period of uncertainty, as the specter of civil war loomed over the country's horizon.

The outbreak of the Civil War in 1860 generally postponed progress in Dubuque, but there were exceptional businesses that profited during wartime. William Ryan, who moved from Galena, Illinois to Dubuque and opened a butcher business while the war raged in the East, was a close friend of Ulysses S. Grant. Ryan, with the endorsement of Grant, secured generous contracts to supply the Union Army with meat rations during the Civil War. As a result, Ryan became the wealthy founder of Dubuque's lucrative meat-packing industry.

Other professions were not so prosperous. Architects had flocked to Dubuque during the 1850s to capitalize on the high demand for building designers. In 1860, fourteen architectural firms were listed in the Dubuque City Directory; by the end of the Civil War, only three of them were left in town. Ironically, those architects that remained in Dubuque experienced an even greater building boom after the sluggish effects of the war economy dissipated.

The Civil War proved to have a deeper financial impact than Dubuque's citizens probably anticipated. Newspaper editorials were optimistic that Union victory would stimulate the economy in the Midwest. To announce the surrender of General Lee's Confederate Army, the bell of the Dubuque First Congregational Church rang all night until it finally cracked at dawn. But like its cracked bell, Dubuque's resources were overtaxed and divided by the end of the war, and it required time and money to repair the damage done.

It took most of the decade for economic conditions and construction activity to regain momentum in Dubuque. As Western expansion increased after the war, entrepreneurs, developers, and builders from the East brought a renewed vitality to Dubuque. These innovators introduced architectural diversity and improvements in construction techniques to the community. By the late 1860s, Dubuque began an intensified urban growth cycle.

During this postwar boom Victorian homes were built in the popular styles of the era, which included interpretations of Italianate, Gothic, and Second Empire motifs. Second Empire homes were particularly popular in Dubuque, because a Mansard-roofed house could be readily adapted to the preferences and income of the builder. Whether built to stand alone or as part of a connected row, the Second Empire residence maintained social acceptance, and its flexible design lent itself equally to a plain exterior treatment or fancy embellishment. This versatility suited the requirements for Dubuque's diverse and distinctive neighborhoods, which symbolized the civic and economic hierarchy of particular groups within the community.

Dubuque's accelerated growth during the early 1870s was interrupted in 1873 by a nationwide financial crisis. Unrestrained stock speculation, overextended land development, and undercapitalized railroad expansion precipitated an economic depression throughout the financial system, which forced local bankers to withhold investments and foreclose construction loans. Midwestern farmers were particularly devastated by a worldwide collapse of the commodities market, which sent wholesale crop prices overseas plummeting.

A. A. Cooper was one of Dubuque's early settlers who became one of the town's most prominent industrialists owning the famed Cooper Wagon Works. The most renowned wagon maker in the West, Cooper Wagon Works was one of the city's largest employers. The Redstone Inn, built in 1894 as a wedding present for his daughter, is the only surviving mansion of Cooper's legacy.

J. K. GRAVES

J K. Graves, who at various points in his career was Dubuque's mayor, most successful banker, and Iowa State Senator, earned another claim to fame by creating the Fenelon Place Elevator. It is the world's steepest, shortest, scenic railway; the cars elevate a few passengers at a time up a sixty-five percent grade measuring two hundred ninety-six feet in length from the business district to the top of the bluffs. Riders are rewarded with a magnificent view across the Mississippi River Valley and into Iowa, Illinois, and Wisconsin.

In 1882 Dubuque was an "hour-and-a-half town"; at noon, businesses closed for ninety minutes while workers went home for their midday meal. Mr. Graves lived on top of the bluffs and commuted to his downtown bank, which meant he spent an hour driving his horse and buggy back up the bluff for his lunch at home. He needed another half hour to return to his office, even though his bank was only two blocks from his house "as the crow flies." By the time Graves made his final trip up the hill at the end of the day, he had spent nearly three hours making two daily round trips!

As a traveler, Graves had seen incline railways in Europe and envisioned a similar system for his neighborhood. He petitioned the city for the right to build an elevator on rails, and the franchise was granted in 1882. A local engineer was hired to design and build a one-car cable modeled after those in the Alps.

The original system, which was built for Mr. Graves' private use, had a small building that housed a coal-fired steam engine boiler and winch. A Swiss-style wooden car was hauled up and down on two rails by a hemp rope and operated for the first time on July 25, 1882. Each business day his gardener let him down in the morning, brought him up at noon, back down after lunch and a nap, and up again at the end of the workday.

In 1884 the elevator burned, when the fire that was banked in the stove for the night raged out of control. After Mr. Graves rebuilt the elevator, his neighbors began asking for rides. He decided to open his service to the public, charging a nickel a ride to defray the cost of operation.

The elevator burned again in 1893. Because there was a recession, Mr. Graves could not afford to rebuild his cable car. Ten neighbors, who had become dependent on the elevator to transport themselves to work, church, and the market, banded together and formed the Fenelon Place Elevator Company. Mr. Graves gave them the franchise for the right-of-way, and the new owners traveled to the 1893 Exposition in Chicago to seek new ideas.

They returned with a streetcar motor to run the elevator, a turnstile, and steel cable for the cars, as each time the elevator house had burned, the hemp rope that held the cable car had burned away and sent it crashing down the hill to destroy the entire operation. They also installed three rails with a bypass track at midpoint that allowed two counter-balanced cars to pass each other in opposite directions.

In 1912 C.B. Trewin, who lived next door to the elevator, became the sole stockholder, after the original ten stockholders either moved or passed away. Mr. Trewin added garages to the north and south sides of the operator's house in 1916. He also added a second floor apartment where the neighborhood men gathered to smoke, play cards, and talk politics.

There was another fire in 1962, caused by an accidental blaze that spread from the operator's room to the upstairs apartment. The cost of repairs raised the ticket price to ten cents a ride! In 1977 the cable cars were completely rebuilt and, after eighty-four years, the original gear drive was replaced by a modern gearbox with a DC motor. To this day Mr. Graves' Fenelon Place Elevator still carries passengers to the top of Dubuque.

This cable car is the only one of its type in the Midwest and is one of three in the nation. The cars travels over a sixty-five percent grade and lift passengers two hundred ninety-six feet. The counterbalanced cars weight sixteen hundred fifty pounds each and are moved by steel cables obtained from the builder of the Brooklyn Bridge. Two motors, a brake lever, a starter, and a turnstile purchased from the 1893 Chicago World's Fair are housed at the top of the bluff.

The recession lasted for most of the decade as public confidence was shaken by political corruption, bankruptcy, and social unrest. By 1880 the country had generally recovered from its worst depression of the century, and cautious idealism replaced unbridled optimism across America. With transcontinental railroad trade firmly established, transportation again linked Dubuque to westward expansion, and the local economy recharged itself by supplying the frontier with highly needed supplies and equipment.

Many Dubuque architects, who had resorted to secondary employment as draftsmen, contractors, surveyors, cabinetmakers, and illustrators during the building slump, returned to their principal occupation during the late 1800s. They designed houses for the wealthy traders, shippers, and manufacturers who profited from Dubuque's role as a Midwestern connection for a bicoastal economy. Queen Anne and Italian Villa homes were popular choices among successful local businessmen, who had their elegant residences built on the bluffs overlooking the Mississippi River.

As a result Dubuque became a two-tiered town, with upper and lower sections divided by the steep escarpments of the Mississippi River Valley. Access to the residential areas above the downtown business district was provided by the construction of "street steps," which were sets of public stairways that offered pedestrian paths for reaching elevated parts of Dubuque. By the turn of the century, over twenty-five different routes led strollers from the "lowlands" to the exclusive neighborhoods along the bluffs.

While upper Dubuque became the fashionable domain of the city's most successful citizens, the core of the local economy remained along the river. The Dubuque Boat and Boiler Works was established on the north shore of Dubuque Harbor in 1906, adjacent to the freight house for the Chicago, Burlington & Northern Railroad. This shipyard enterprise built sea and river vessels for the United States Navy, which supplied Dubuque with substantial government contracts during the first half of the twentieth-century. Dubuque's most famous ship, the U.S.S. Sprague, was nicknamed "Big Mama," and after extensive World War battle duty it was converted into a floating museum in Vicksburg, Mississippi.

After World War II the vintage Victorian homes that epitomized another era were no longer fashionable with homeowners of the 1950s. In the name of modernization, traditional turrets were torn down, textured wooden walls were covered with aluminum siding, and intricate ornamentation was stripped to eliminate any exterior detail that was purely

Patterned shingling is the hallmark of this Queen Anne family home built in 1891, for one of the local merchants. Queen Anne designs invite curiosity and intrigue with numerous features such as dramatic balconies, inglenooks, crannies, attics, basements, stained glass windows and towers.

Four major financial panics struck the United States during the 1800s. The entire country felt the impact of these economic upheavals to some extent, and Dubuque was particularly paralyzed by financial forces that operated beyond its own control. Like many trade-oriented towns, Dubuque's progress in the nineteenth- century was directly linked to the general condition of the national economy, which suffered a major crisis about every twenty years during the Victorian Era.

Panic of 1837

Following an unprecedented period of land speculation, canal excavation, and railroad construction, the reckless behavior of private investors compelled the federal government to refuse letters of credit for the purchase of public lands. The panic began when President Jackson, during his last year in office (1836), issued his "Specie Circular" that ordered the Federal Treasury to refuse private bank notes as collateral for buying public property. American entrepreneurs already owed enormous debts to British bankers, who had loaned large sums of European capital to fund wildcat financial schemes in the United States.

When the federal government suspended credit to private banks, the British were forced to call in their overseas loans, which caused the bankruptcy of many under-capitalized businesses in America. Bank failures mounted, inflation soared, and unemployment became rampant. Economic distress continued for several years until conservative fiscal policies implemented by the federal government restored a viable balance between private investment and public funding.

Panic of 1857

After the conquests of the Mexican War opened the Southwest to American expansion, unbridled land speculation and opportunistic railroad development fueled almost a decade of unchecked economic growth in the United States. Many poorly regulated banks overextended themselves to finance high-risk frontier ventures that jeopardized their capital assets. When interest rates soared and investment loans became unattractive, the economy slid into a cyclical recession in response to its tight money supply.

In 1857 the failure of the Ohio Life Insurance Company in Cincinnati touched off a regional panic, which quickly spread nationwide and severely curtailed industrial development in the East and agricultural growth in the Midwest. The Panic of 1857 precipitated unemployment, labor unrest, and sectionalism between the North and South. As civil war seemed imminent, interstate commerce diminished, regional trade became sporadic, and the nation's productivity stagnated. After the Civil War, the federal government tried to revitalize the economy with federal funding for Western expansion.

Panic of 1873

Efforts by the federal government to stimulate Western expansion included lucrative land grants and low-interest loans to railroad companies. Indiscriminate railroad construction and unregulated business practices allowed the railroad magnates to exploit the generosity of the Congress at the expense of the American public. The financial structure of the United States was manipulated by robber barons, whose personal exploits caused currency inflation, trade imbalance of imports over exports, and economic chaos for private enterprise.

The failure of Jay Cooke's prestigious banking house in 1873 stirred a panic among fellow financiers on Wall Street. The ten-day closing of the New York Stock Exchange was followed by the worst depression the nation had yet experienced. More than eighteen thousand businesses failed during the next few years, many regional railroads went into bankruptcy, and unemployment far outstripped the ability of charity to relieve hunger and destitution. A strike by railroad workers in 1877 brought violence and federal intervention to the labor movement, and a symbolic rift between the working and ruling classes was created. The general welfare began to improve by 1878, but tension, uncertainty, and mistrust continued to influence the American economy.

Panic of 1893

The tenuous nature of the American economy in the 1800s made it particularly vulnerable to external influences such as international banking, balance-of-trade, and foreign commodities. A spectacular financial crisis erupted in 1893 when the majority of European securities investments were suddenly recalled from the United States by nervous overseas bankers. When these investors liquidated their shares from the New York Stock Market, the abandoned Wall Street community collapsed. Domestic gold supplies were depleted, because the American dollar was cashed in for gold on foreign commodities markets. Furthermore, the Sherman Silver Act allowed silver certificate holders to redeem their money for its equivalent value in gold.

The decline in the Federal Treasury's gold reserve affected a drop in the international prices of gold, silver and other commodities. As bank reserves devalued in the United States, a recessionary cycle of business failures, unemployment, and depression plagued the national economy. The repeal of the Sherman Silver Act returned the American dollar to the gold standard, and many businesses that had silver investments were forced into bankruptcy due to the devaluation of silver ore. Other struggling companies were merged to form larger consumer and manufacturing conglomerates, and as they entered the industrialized twentieth-century as huge corporations, the American economy had also transformed itself to survive and compete within the changing world marketplace.

Historically, the German and Irish communities were not known for their brotherly love. It seems somewhat ironic that the German congregation of St. Mary's Church with its two hundred thirty foot spire was designed by one of Dubuque's Irish architects.

European craftsmen from England, Ireland, and Scotland, as well as American tradesmen from the East Coast, were among the artisans that moved to Dubuque and spent many years applying their skills as brick masons, stonecutters and master builder carpenters.

decorative. Minimalism replaced flamboyance, and conservatism prevailed over extravagance. Americans drearily took the fun out of their architecture.

Fortunately, Dubuque, which is faithfully tied to local culture and tradition, has evolved from its previous economic base of agriculture, meat-packing, and ship-building to more diversified enterprises such as custom furniture making, electronics, and tourism. As new people and markets have come to Dubuque a renewed interest in its eclectic architecture has emerged. Although Dubuque has expanded to sixteen times its size of only a century ago, it still retains the small town atmosphere that inspires historical preservation.

Today there are well-preserved Victorians in Dubuque that house bed-and-breakfast inns, restaurants, and traditional family businesses. Along the riverfront, visitors can see "The William Black," one of the largest paddlewheelers still in existence, and experience the Woodward Riverboat Museum, which portrays life along the Mississippi River during the last two centuries. Best of all, historical enthusiasts can ride through the tree-lined neighborhoods of Dubuque in guided horse-drawn carriages and admire tasteful examples of virtually every major style in American Victorian architecture. Dubuque truly remains a town of "Victorian Variety."

The etched glass door lights in the front entry of the current Ryan House Restaurant attest to the lavish taste of its first owner. It was designed by Fridolin Heer and built in 1870 for John Thompson, a Civil War mayor of Dubuque. Thompson was a prominent leather merchant who, like Ryan, made his fortune during the Civil War. He was also a friend and business associate of U.S. Grant and Grant's father, a leather merchant in Galena. The Thompsons entertained the Grants in their gracious home several times.

William Ryan and his brother James operated a wholesale grocery business in Galena. The Ryan brothers enjoyed a favorable connection with their Galena friend, General U.S. Grant, which resulted in their receiving large and continuing orders to supply pork for the Army. In 1868, William moved to Dubuque to establish his own meat-packing business that earned him a fortune through his foresight and efforts. William Ryan purchased this home in 1888 for his second wife and their six children.

Left: **These two homes, with their tall belvederes topped with cast-iron cresting, were originally thirteen feet closer to each other. Both were once owned by William Ryan; the house on the right was the home of his first wife and their seven children. He remarried after his wife passed away and lived next door with his second wife and their six children. To afford more privacy between the houses, he had the house on the left moved off its foundation and over thirteen feet.**

Right: **Spires, towers and domes of varying architectural styles span an architectural legacy celebrating the glory of this interesting port town.**

DUBUQUE, *Victorian Variety*

ST. LOUIS

Gateway to the West

THE VICTORIAN EXPRESS

ST. LOUIS
MISSOURI

ALL ABOARD EXCURSION

TRAIN NO.	CAR	TICKET NO.	RES. NO.
91	FIRST CLASS	008	288

PASSENGER RECEIPT

DESTINATION

St. Louis was the "Gateway to the West" for explorers, trappers, miners, pioneers and immigrants. Many westward-bound settlers started their journey at the site of the Old Court House, which is framed today by the St. Louis Arch.

St. Louis has always been at the center of American expansionism. Explorers chose it as their point of departure into the uncharted Western wilderness. Trappers and traders met at the confluence of its rivers to exchange their goods. European nations attempted to make it a symbolic outpost for their territorial empires. Pioneers immigrated from the North, East, and South to populate its domain. Settlers harvested its pastures, forests, and minerals. Politicians debated its political impact upon a divided country. Entrepreneurs developed boat and rail transportation to make it a trade center. The story of St. Louis in many ways portrays the evolution of the American frontier.

When Pierre Liguest Laclede arrived in New Orleans from France in 1755, he formed a partnership with trader Antoine Maxent to promote new business along the Mississippi River. They obtained permission from the French Governor-General of New Orleans to negotiate an exclusive trading agreement with the Osage and Missouri Indians. The traders proposed to establish an upriver trade settlement near the French military stronghold, Fort de Chartes, which was strategically located on the east bank of the Mississippi River.

In August 1763 Laclede led a precarious flotilla of boats and rafts up the Mississippi to find an appropriate building site for their trading post. Meanwhile, Louis XV had relinquished control of French territory east of the Mississippi to the British as a treaty concession at the end of the Seven Years' War, so Laclede was instructed to select a location on the west bank. By December, the landing party had reached the confluence of the Missouri and Mississippi Rivers, where Laclede chose an ideal site for construction.

The men built their settlement on a high bluff to avert danger from seasonal river flooding; they relied on a nearby stream for water, which quenched their thirst and propelled a water mill. An ample supply of timber and limestone provided the necessary construction materials, and a fertile prairie extended westward for growing crops and pasturing animals. Laclede christened his settlement "Saint Louis," in honor of King Louis XV and the monarch's patron saint, King Louis IX.

In 1762 Louis XV secretly transferred to Charles III of Spain "the country known by the name of Louisiana," which included the Missouri territory where St. Louis stood. France had suffered economically from its lengthy war with England, and the administration of the Louisiana Territory placed an additional financial burden on the French treasury. In 1770 the Spanish Crown officially assumed control of the region west of the Mississippi for a combination of economic and political reasons.

Spain hoped that the Louisiana Territory might reveal precious metals similar to its silver-producing claims in the Southwest. The Spanish also feared further English exploration and development west of the Mississippi, so they considered Louisiana and Missouri a political buffer zone against British encroachment. Spanish Americans were encouraged to resettle near St. Louis outside the domain of British taxation and religious persecution.

After the Revolutionary War, defeated English-American Tories left their homes in states like Kentucky, Tennessee, and Virginia to seek refuge in St. Louis. French and English immigrants also came south from Canada to live in Missouri. St. Louis became the capital of Upper Louisiana, and Spain signed a treaty with the United States in 1795 to open trade routes along the Mississippi River, which dramatically increased American immigration.

Spanish-controlled Louisiana and Missouri rewarded settlers with free land grants, no taxes, and religious tolerance. As St. Louis grew in size and municipal expense, Spain began to weigh the benefit of permanently establishing its presence in North America against the increasing cost of governing the tax-free territory. By 1800 Spain had become financially overextended, and it returned possession of Missouri to France at the request of Napoleon, who entertained grandiose thoughts of creating a French empire in North America.

The United States became increasingly resentful of attempts by the English, Spanish, and French to dominate the American frontier west of the Mississippi. President Thomas Jefferson sent a diplomatic envoy to France with instructions to negotiate a land settlement that would diminish European interference with American trade on the Mississippi. In 1803

This home was built 1873 for the large family of a successful German immigrant. It was sold in 1890 to new owners, who had their roof blown off by the 1896 tornado. After the tornado's devastation, the roof was remodeled to suggest its current style, with parapeted gables, a rare but characteristic feature of the Queen Anne style. Since 1915, the thirty-two-room mansion has served as a funeral home.

Napoleon fulfilled Jefferson's greatest expectations when he agreed to sell over a million square miles of the Louisiana Territory to the United States for fifteen million dollars.

In what was certainly the most vital real estate deal in American history, the Louisiana Purchase unleashed American westward expansion. Jefferson hoped for a gradual development of Missouri that would allow the resident Indian tribes sufficient time to experience a peaceful integration into American culture. The president sought to stabilize internal conflict in the West by peaceful coexistence with native Americans. He believed that the Indian presence on the Western frontier would deter further attempts by the Spanish and English to control these territories.

The Louisiana Purchase stipulated, however, that the transfer of the French territory to the United States required those settlers west of the Mississippi to immediately become American citizens, or the agreement would be rescinded. Napoleon began to regret his decision to sell the Louisiana and Missouri Territories, and he hoped that the citizenship issue would abrogate the land deal. Jefferson understood the political jeopardy involved, and he hastened Congress to quickly ratify the treaty.

With congressional approval safely achieved, Jefferson decided to appraise the

Left: **This home, first completed in 1878 as the residence for a milling company owner, later became both home and office for a doctor around the turn of the century. His surgical sink still remains in the first floor bath. The exterior palette was inspired by the fall colors in Lafayette Park.**

Right: **Horace E. Bixby, a riverboat pilot who taught Mark Twain how to navigate the Mississippi River for five hundred dollars, was the original owner of this house. Riverboat captains were dashing figures, big spenders, and popular with St. Louis belles. Captain Bixby was no exception to this reputation, and after boarding with a local family, he married their daughter and bought her this home in 1877.**

value of his country's illustrious land acquisition. In 1804 he commissioned the team of Meriwether Lewis and William Clark to organize an expedition to ascertain what opportunities awaited to the west of St. Louis. For over two years, the intrepid Lewis and Clark expedition traversed the American West in search of the fabled Northwest Passage, hoping to link St. Louis to profitable markets in the Orient.

As Lewis and Clark began their famous journey from St. Louis up the Missouri River, they fully expected to find an easy route that would enable traders to efficiently transport American goods to Pacific markets and vice versa. When they returned to St. Louis in 1806 to recount their incredible experiences, the explorers told dismayed merchants that no easy passage to the West Coast had been found over the formidable Rockies. But Lewis and Clark did enthusiastically report that the opportunities for mining, trapping, and trading within the territory were unlimited.

In 1808 the Missouri Fur Company was established in St. Louis to handle the growing influx of business supplied from trappers working the Northern wilderness. Lead mining became popular in Missouri, and St. Louis was the trading center for equipment and supplies. Dozens of general stores and specialty shops opened along Main Street to serve the burgeoning city population.

Left: **French Second Empire's hallmark characteristic is the predominant Mansard sloping roof. In contrast to the traditional convex and concave curves used in many Mansard designs, the houses located around Lafayette Square mostly have straight roof slopes.**

Right: **Lafayette Square's Annual Home Tours draws thousands of participants. Each year a different poster is created, and one recent poster featured close-up photographs of each home's entry doors.**

THOMAS HART BENTON

Originally from Hillsboro, North Carolina, Thomas Hart Benton moved west to St. Louis in 1815 to practice law and become editor of the *Missouri Enquirer*. As a strong advocate for American expansion, Benton used his newspaper status to publicize his views favoring the acquisition of the Texas, California, and Oregon territories for statehood. He proposed land grants for settlers, but he loathed land speculators, and his editorials gained him political support.

Nominated to the Senate by the son of Daniel Boone, Benton was first elected to the United States Congress in 1820. As a Senator from Missouri, he became involved almost immediately in his lifelong legislative interest, national fiscal responsibility. Always a "hard money" man, he endorsed the distribution of currency redeemable for gold and silver, but he disapproved of paper notes issued by uninsured banks.

He supported President Andrew Jackson's national policy to finance the purchase of public lands with money secured by the Federal Reserve. When the financial panic of 1837 forced many undercapitalized banks to close, Benton suggested that federal banking regulations be enacted. He legislated for federal land grants to the railroads, which he hoped would stimulate the deflated economy and facilitate the construction of a transcontinental railroad route through St. Louis.

Benton advocated the navigational charting of the Mississippi River, and he promoted the construction of a highway to New Mexico following the Santa Fe Trail. His aggressive attitude towards westward development was inspired by the explorations of his son-in-law, John C. Fremont, who had personally charted much of the Western wilderness. Benton also supported funding for the Pony Express, a national telegraph network, and a coast-to-coast railroad network, with its hub in St. Louis.

Although Benton's fiscal and growth policies were well received, Missourians resented their Senator's defection on the major issue of slavery. Benton was essentially a racial moderate, and he was willing to live without slavery to avoid civil war. Because of his loyalty to the federal government, Benton refused to support secession, and he voted for the admission of California to the Union as a free state. When he opposed the Compromise of 1850, which would have made California half-slave and half-free, he offended his Missouri constituents beyond reelection.

With his political career sacrificed, Thomas Hart Benton retired from Congress and returned to St. Louis to write his memoirs. A ten-foot bronze figure was erected in Lafayette Park in 1868 to commemorate his life.

Attention to detail is the standard that aptly describes the time and effort invested to showcase the intricate exterior embellishments of Victorian homes.

By 1815 commercial activity in St. Louis was flourishing. The city acted as trade center between Eastern civilization and the Western frontier. Finished goods were distributed from suppliers on the East Coast, while raw materials from the West were shipped to manufacturers along the Eastern seaboard and in Europe. The first steamboats successfully reached St. Louis in 1817, and for decades from then on a constant stream of riverboats carried passengers and cargo between the busy ports of St. Louis and New Orleans.

Southern commerce also introduced slavery and plantation attitudes to St. Louis. When Missouri applied for acceptance into the Union in 1819, it catalyzed a conflict among the other twenty-two states, which were evenly divided on the practice of slavery. In a political compromise, Missouri was allowed to join the Union as a slave state, while Maine was annexed from upper Massachusetts to create an additional free state. Congress legislated the Missouri Compromise, which stated that slavery would be excluded from territory acquired by the Louisiana Purchase located north of 36° 30'.

With statehood established, St. Louis incorporated in 1822, and civic leaders began to create a master plan for integrating the city's residential growth and commercial expansion into an effective urban network. By 1836, St. Louis authorities had reserved thirty acres of municipally held land for a "public square," which created the first city park west of the Mississippi. This parcel of land had originally been reserved for pastureland as part of the St. Louis Commons, and as "Lafayette Park" it remains the only land within the city that has never been privately owned.

The next several years brought tumultuous changes to St. Louis. Financial panic distressed local investors in 1837, when a federal currency crisis limited the availability of venture capital for several years. The town was also disrupted by the War with Mexico during the early 1840s, because many local businessmen were commercially involved with the outcome of the conflict through their Southwestern trading connections. Furthermore, the discovery of gold in California compelled another group of eager entrepreneurs to liquidate their local businesses and join the rush towards the Pacific Coast.

Besides these economic curtailments, the wooden wharves of the St. Louis waterfront were decimated by an uncontrollable fire in the spring of 1849. Before the ashes had cooled, a cholera epidemic plagued the city, which robbed the lives of several thousand defenseless St. Louisians. During a disastrous decade, the "mistress of the Mississippi" was consecutively impoverished, forsaken, and devastated by misfortune.

The panels gracing the entrances to these Victorian town houses were given a more dimensional quality, by using a contrasting pattern of light and dark colors to add depth to the twin entry doors.

Despite its setbacks, St. Louis continued to grow dramatically in the 1850s. A ten-year census revealed that between the cataclysmic years of 1840 and 1850, the city population had nevertheless quadrupled. With its rapid growth to over ninety thousand town residents, St. Louis became "the Gateway to the West," as new settlers cruised by boats from the South, rode trains from the East, and ventured westward by wagon on the Santa Fe Trail.

The migratory flow of people to St. Louis brought financial prosperity for local merchants, who profited as wholesalers, traders, and suppliers to the marketplace. The most successful businessmen and town leaders built lavish residences along Lafayette Park, which had developed into the city's most prestigious neighborhood. Lafayette Park earned a local reputation as a place where, according to the *Daily Evening News*, "Every dwelling is a model of tasty architecture and every yard a charming grove."

Homeowners along the square matched city funds to improve the Park and finance the construction of an outdoor concert garden. In January 1859 the first professional concert was performed in the "New Winter Garden" for an admission fee of fifteen cents. With the outbreak of the Civil War, St. Louis was placed under Union martial law, and civic improvements were generally postponed during the war

180

Left: **In 1884, the construction company of Andrew Uhri & Sons built this townhouse for Mr. Uhri's personal residence. Uhri's busy firm eventually built seven more Victorians on the same street.**

Right: **Hundreds of different door designs were featured in millshop publications across the country, and their styles frequently changed to keep pace with the newest trends in house plans. Even the most intricately carved doors were offered through these catalogs with prices ranging from two to twelve dollars.**

years. The park reputedly served as a secret rendezvous for St. Louis families of Southern sympathies and Confederate soldiers engaged in nearby conflicts.

Following the Civil War, Lafayette Park became enormously popular with the nouveau riche and politically powerful citizens of St. Louis. The neighborhood elite included the City Mayor, the President of the American Bar Association, two United States Congressmen, one United States Senator, four members of the Presidential Cabinet, and one Supreme Court Justice. On May 27, 1868, a crowd of twenty thousand admirers gathered in Lafayette Park to watch Mrs. John C. Fremont unveil a bronze statue of her famous father, St. Louis Senator Thomas Hart Benton.

By 1870 Lafayette Park was a conspicuously luxurious place to live. An exclusive fence with marble gateposts was constructed around the two-mile perimeter of the Park at a cost of fifty thousand dollars. Private cul-de-sacs and drives were lined with elegant town houses constructed in the popular Second Empire style of the era. The stylish Mansard roof, popular in Eastern cities such as Philadelphia, was simultaneously introduced to St. Louis on a mansion built for locally prominent businessman, and many subsequent residences were adorned with the chic Mansard look.

Left: **Dramatic usage of color has become the distinguishing characteristic of many Lafayette Square homes. Here the vibrant and exuberant combination of pastel colors calls immediate attention to the details, surfaces, and scale of this entrance.**

Right: **Doors, windows, and their surrounding treatments were readily available from the millshops of the nineteenth-century. The semi-circular "eyebrows," that crown the doors and windows of this Lafayette Square home, had to be molded by hand during a recent, extensive remodeling.**

The history of Lafayette Square began in 1836, when city land was set aside for a public park and square for recreational purposes. This tree-lined tract was officially named "Lafayette Square" in honor of the French General, the Marquis de Lafayette.

AN AFTERNOON AT THE PARK

By 1873 weekly outdoor concerts in Lafayette Park had become a popular part of the St. Louis social scene. Thousands of resident attended the Thursday afternoon performances during the summer months. Newcomers to St. Louis also found excursions to the Park quite entertaining, as described by this Memphis visitor: "Walking down Fourth Street the other day, I was much interested in the conversation of two ladies in front of me, when all at once one of them exclaimed: 'There is a Lafayette Park car, let's go out — it's concert day.'

"Since I have been trying to 'do' this village for some time, I thought it would be quite the thing for me to go out to the Park too. I hailed the next car, but of course the driver was not looking my way, and though I moved my fan frequently, that man was fully determined not to stop. I think he must have been more interested in his mule from the way he stared at it.

"I waited until the next car came in sight, and then I walked out to the middle of the street and 'histed' my parasol by way of signaling. I stuck my parasol out and pushed it up and down several times in rapid succession, and that driver's mule stopped. It was a warm day and the ride was delightful. We had a long ride to Choteau Avenue, and after getting off the track several times, finally arrived at my destination.

"I followed the crowd through the gate and up the walk which was rather rough, so I took to the grass. Hearing music in the distance, I kept on going and finally stopped, entranced. Talk about dreamland! There were gorgeous flowers, fountains, playing; the grass like velvet, sweet music, and sitting or walking, the beauty and fashion of this grand old city, flitting in and out among the trees, rustic bridges and grottoes. There is a miniature lake with swans and ducks floating around; and for a five-cent fare you can take a ride in a pretty boat, three times around the lake. Altogether I spent a delightful afternoon."

After the concerts, strolling spectators visited statues of Senator Benton and George Washington as well as viewed the three ship's cannons taken from a British Man o' War sunk in 1776. Immaculate Victorian homes lined the park perimeter and completed a scene of carefree elegance as socialites boarded their carriages for the leisurely ride home.

Life in Lafayette Park epitomized the Victorian Era in St. Louis. Gleaming carriages lined the one-hundred-foot-wide avenues outside the Park, while sightseers enjoyed shaded comfort amidst thirty acres of impeccable landscaping, gardens, and ponds. Respectable matrons with ruffled parasols and whalebone-corseted dresses strolled the groomed paths to admire each other's fashionable attire, while gentlemen of distinction congregated to smoke cigars and debate the issues of the day. By the end of the nineteenth-century, St. Louis had established itself as a showcase for the region's rich and famous, and Laclede's rustic trading post had evolved into America's sixth largest city.

Tragedy struck Lafayette Square on May 27, 1896, when a cyclone swept a deadly path of destruction across the pristine neighborhood. Within minutes of impact, the stoic, stately homes of Lafayette Park were torn apart like matchboxes in a blender. Huge trees in the park were snapped like toothpicks, and excursion boats were thrown hundreds of feet like toys in a tub. The two-mile fence around the park was flattened, the ornamental bandstand leveled, and several neighborhood churches crashed to the ground. Worst of all, many of the city's most beloved citizens were instantly lost.

Most former homeowners could not

stand the grief of rebuilding their houses from the rubble, so they left the remnants of Lafayette Square behind and resettled elsewhere. Others tried to restore the previous appearance of their lost churches and homes by faithfully following their original construction plans, but these efforts were largely in vain, because the time, money, and expertise required for renovation was overwhelming. Those who chose to persevere in the aftermath spent the remainder of their lives haunted by the presence of the cyclone's devastation.

Most of the surviving buildings in Lafayette Square were eventually abandoned over the next fifty years and declined into gradual disrepair. Some of the larger mansions were divided into multiple-family dwellings during the city's lean economic years. Other Victorian victims simply fell before the wrecking ball under the pretense of "progress," "urban renewal," and "modernization." By the end of the 1950s, Lafayette Square had degenerated into a disreputable district on the south side of St. Louis.

In the 1960s a new group of urban pioneers returned to Lafayette Square to rekindle a romance with its architectural tradition. The Lafayette Square Restoration Committee was formed to organize and support efforts for historic renovation in the neighborhood. The members have reclaimed dozens of vintage homes and lovingly restored these residences to their original grandeur.

In 1972 the Lafayette Square Restoration Committee was rewarded for its efforts towards architectural preservation, when the City of St. Louis officially declared Lafayette Square its first historic district. The United States Congress endorsed this status in 1973 when it placed Lafayette Square on the National Register of Historic Places. By 1975 municipal funds were allocated to landscape the park and renovate historic buildings located on public property.

Since that time, annual home tours have introduced thousands of visitors to the residential renaissance of Lafayette Square. St. Louis enthusiasts are selling their modern suburban homes to reinvest in traditional downtown Victorians as their primary residences. Summer concerts and social events are again held in the Park, and a sense of community has revitalized the neighborhood with antique shops, specialty stores, and intimate restaurants. A "small town within the city" has brought Lafayette Park and St. Louis together for their mutual survival.

St. Louis has experienced many incarnations: from trading post to trade center, from political pawn to principal power, from humble hamlet to metropolitan Mecca. Throughout these dramatic changes the citizens of St. Louis have welcomed newcomers to their city as partners in opportunity. This open civic attitude towards growth and progress has rewarded the city with many accomplishments. Most importantly, St. Louis has established its historical tradition of leading America towards new frontiers and rightfully deserves to be called the "Gateway to the West."

Architectural and aesthetic unity has been achieved in this detailed cornice by the subtle use color transitions in the swags and bull's-eyes that enhance its crisp design.

TOPEKA

Railroad Rendezvous

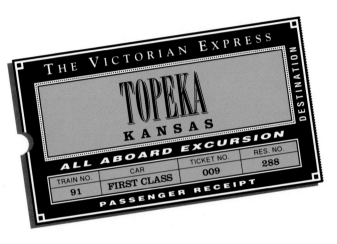

THE VICTORIAN EXPRESS

TOPEKA
KANSAS

ALL ABOARD EXCURSION

TRAIN NO.	CAR	TICKET NO.	RES. NO.
91	FIRST CLASS	009	288

PASSENGER RECEIPT

DESTINATION

This quilt was handmade by the residents of Potwin Place to celebrate their Centennial in 1987, when it was displayed in Topeka's Kansas Museum of History. Potwin Place is a unique neighborhood with brick streets and circular parks at street intersections. Charles Potwin planted two thousand elm trees and allowed them to mature before permitting house construction. This astute businessman understood the value of creating the friendly neighborhood environment that remains in Potwin Place today.

Topeka, Kansas, since its inception, has always been a transportation center. As American expansion swept westward across the nation in the nineteenth-century, Topeka served as a popular hub for travel and commerce between the Eastern establishment and the Western frontier. To this day major railroads use Topeka as a distribution center for their Midwestern train traffic, and the Santa Fe Railroad remains an important factor in the local economy.

The name "Topeka" has several possible origins. Thomas Say, a scientist who accompanied an exploratory expedition through the Kansas territory in 1819, described an Otoe Indian name for the Kansas River as "to-pe-ka," which he translated as "good potato river." In the Kansa Indian language, "Topeka" referred to "a good place to dig potatoes," and local tribes used the term to describe what is now the Smoky Hill riverfront area.

Those descriptions matched the discoveries of Cyrus K. Holliday, who led a group of settlers up the Kansas River valley to establish a new town in 1854, after the federal government officially declared the Kansas Territory open for land development. Holliday and his party located a townsite along the river, which had plentiful water and provided an accessible landing for steamboats. Furthermore, there were ample building materials such as stone, sand, and timber for developing their new home, christened "Topeka."

In December 1854 Holliday sent his wife a letter, headed "Topeka, K.T.," that described the deplorable conditions of his first winter in a makeshift prairie cabin: "What we have to endure is almost beyond belief — it is a long time since I have seen anything in the shape of a bed. I have a buffalo robe and two blankets in which I roll myself and lie down to rest upon the bare ground with boots, hat, overcoat, and all on. Our food is mush, molasses, and bacon, mixed plentifully with dirt three times each day. Thus we live in Kansas."

While the original founders of Topeka endured the winter of 1854, debate continued in the United States Congress over the destiny of Kansas. Earlier in the year, Senator Stephen Douglas of Illinois had secured passage of the Kansas-Nebraska Act, which proclaimed the territories west of Iowa and Missouri as Nebraska and Kansas. To gain Southern support in the Senate, Douglas agreed to vote for the repeal of the Missouri Compromise, thereby making it politically possible for Kansas to enter the Union as a slave state if Nebraska joined as a slave-free state.

In a political process known as popular sovereignty, Congress allowed Kansas leaders to petition their territorial residents and measure the majority opinion whether slavery should exist in their new state. Slave owners from Missouri infiltrated the Kansas caucus in Lecompton and outvoted abolitionists to enact a Constitution that guaranteed slavery with Kansas statehood. Angry antislavery settlers refused to recognize the legitimacy of the Lecompton Constitution, so they formed an alternative state government that rivaled the protagonists of slavery for power.

As a congressional deadlock between

Left: **Some of the earlier residents that sat on this porch were railroad men, such as A.A. Robinson, Chief Engineer and Vice President of the Atchison, Topeka & Santa Fe Railroad. W.H. Stillwell occupied this home after 1892; he was the Assistant General Superintendent of the Rock Island Lines, west of the Missouri River.**

Right: **A Topeka Capital reporter, after a stroll through Potwin Place in September 1887 reported: "Mr. S.K. Cross is building a very handsome new frame residence." This Italianate house, the only one of its kind in Potwin Place, features a rare maritime "widow's walk" on the roof. This is a curious feature for a Kansas house located thousands of miles from the nearest ocean.**

pro-slavery Democrats and free-state Republicans polarized and paralyzed the issue of Kansas statehood, factional fighting and bloodshed erupted for several years, branding the troubled territory with the nickname, "Bleeding Kansas." Increasing sectionalism over the slavery issue exacerbated civil unrest for several years, until an uneasy peace finally exploded into the Civil War. In a nation that was divided over slavery, towns like Topeka fell into turmoil.

During the 1860s Topeka became the political center of Kansas. As the seat of Shawnee County, Topeka prevailed over the rival towns of Tecumseh and Lawrence to be chosen as the new state capital in 1861. After the war, Topeka's capital status attracted attention and investment from developers. Churches, schools, and Washburn College were established to cater to the increased influx of sophisticated Eastern families.

The railroads in particular saw potential for using Topeka as a central juncture within their network of regional lines. Entrepreneurs like town-founder Cyrus Holliday created the Atchison, Topeka, and Santa Fe Railway, and within the decade a new Southwest railroad route was well under construction. The headquarters and train shops for the Santa Fe were located in Topeka, where they have remained in operation ever since.

The Union Pacific Railroad also recognized the value of Topeka for its operations, and in 1865 express trains from the East began to arrive, carrying passengers and cargo en route to the Western frontier. By 1869 the Union Pacific and Santa Fe cooperatively handled train traffic between the Northeast and Southwest, and a transcontinental link with Southern Pacific Railroad through New Mexico was planned. National train transit flourished, and Topeka became the railroad rendezvous of Kansas.

By 1870 Topeka seemed headed for prosperity. The small prairie town began to attract speculators, who opened hotels, banks, publishing firms, and a variety of services to support the railroad economy. At the same time, the city sold municipal bonds to provide capital for local industrial development of such projects as the Topeka Iron and Steel Company and the King Wrought Iron Bridge factory. Additionally, cottage industries including cigar producers, flour mills, and breweries emerged on the scene.

Except for a few urban areas, Kansas in the 1870s was essentially an agricultural state, and the financial security of Kansas was intrinsically linked to the economic condition of its farms. While cities such as Topeka experienced a transportation and building boom after the Civil War, the rural majority of Kansas fell victim to three consecutive forces that curtailed agricultural

growth: the economic depression of 1873, the drought of 1874, and the grasshopper plague of 1875.

The Financial Panic of 1873 caused the failure of many banks across America, including the First National Bank of Topeka, which had provided Kansas farmers with low-interest loans to start their farms. After capital funds dried up, the water supply also evaporated in the worst drought the Plains had suffered since Kansas became a farming region. Finally, vast clouds of grasshoppers decimated the scant crops of wheat, rye, and corn to leave a storm-like path of total devastation across Kansas fields.

The economic catastrophes of the Kansas farmbelt affected the quality of life in Topeka as well. The state and city governments lost substantial tax revenue when many farms and businesses were forced into bankruptcy. Public programs for health, safety, and education were either canceled or curtailed until the municipal economy could revitalize itself.

Less than half of Topeka's eligible children were provided with a public education in the 1870s, due to a lack of teachers, facilities, and programs. Teachers' salaries were too low to attract qualified candidates from outside Topeka. Only one new building was erected for educational purposes during the decade; this forced many classes to be conducted in private homes, churches, and borrowed public buildings. No curriculum existed to guide teachers in the proper selection of teaching materials.

Fortunately for Topeka, the railroad business survived the decade and brought renewed prosperity to Kansas in the 1880s. Because the railroads received construction loans and free "buffer zone" land grants from the federal government to encourage the development of new rail lines, the railroad companies acquired extensive tracts of grazing land across the country. Cattle raising proved to be a lucrative spin-off business for the railroads, which used much of their profits to purchase more city land.

As a railroad town, Topeka witnessed an unprecedented real estate boom in the 1880s. Subdivisions sprang up around the periphery of Topeka, ready for another onslaught of speculators, developers, and entrepreneurs to resettle in Kansas. One such community was called Potwin Place, which began with one man's dream to create an exclusive, prestigious neighborhood on the outskirts of Topeka.

In 1882 Charles W. Potwin, originally

This Potwin Place home, built in 1887, typifies the popular "Stick" style that prevailed in this Topeka neighborhood. Local homeowners relied mostly on color variations to lend individuality to their structurally similar Victorian residences.

from Zanesville, Ohio, decided to subdivide a seventy-acre tract of farmland west of Topeka, which he had purchased over a decade before for fourteen thousand four hundred dollars from a Shawnee half-breed named Alexander Beauchemie. Potwin parceled his property into eighty residential lots, each measuring one hundred twenty-two by two hundred five feet. He positioned the homesites along elm-lined cobblestone streets, with a circular park in the middle of each intersection.

Potwin began to sell lots in 1885 with the stipulation that builders had to spend at least two thousand dollars on their new homes. To Potwin's delight, the first six residences were built at a cost of at least five thousand dollars each. In 1888 Potwin Place was incorporated as a separate township from Topeka, which gave the new neighborhood an exclusive quality as well as a convenient tax exemption from Topeka collectors. The City of Potwin Place grew to over six hundred citizens by 1889, as social status seekers eagerly moved into the trendy neighborhood. Many of Topeka's most successful businessmen and civic leaders purchased homes in Potwin Place, where their wives and families enjoyed an aristocratic agenda of social, cultural, and recreational events.

Potwin Place became such an integral aspect of Topeka's lifestyle that the two

The first three titleholders of this house, built in 1887, were all women. One of these female home-owners used the residence as a boarding house in the 1890s.

Right: **This gracious home, with its cool shade trees and inviting porches, was the location for Potwin Place's first wedding, held in 1889.**

cities planned to merge their combined total of over thirty-five thousand residents by the end of the decade. Greater Topeka dominated Kansas as the political, economic, and cultural capital of the state. With its increased size, power, and prestige, however, came a responsibility to lead the state through tough challenges ahead. Again, Topeka faced possible fiscal failure due to forces beyond its control.

The railroads, which had stimulated heavy investment in Topeka real estate and local businesses during the 1880s, began to falter. Kansas farm production had suffered when bankers shifted their capital investment from farm loans to real estate acquisition in cities like Topeka. As crop volumes diminished, railroad profits from freight income also decreased. Railroad owners fell behind on their government loans as cash flow became tight. To make matters worse, labor unrest over unfair management practices forced railroad representatives to negotiate costly settlements with disgruntled rail workers.

The railroads' real estate investments in Topeka depreciated rapidly in value due to an over-abundance of residential subdivisions and insufficient financing. According to city assessment records, the appraised value of Topeka real estate fell from over ten million dollars in 1890 to less than two million dollars by 1892. As the housing

The most infamous railroad magnate was Jay Gould, a financier, gambler, and tycoon, who could make or break a railroad with his power. While still in his teens, Gould entered the lucrative leather trade, where his financial success led him quickly to the investment world of Wall Street. He became a millionaire before he was twenty-one, but he lost his first fortune during the Panic of 1857 in a costly lesson about the risks of speculation.

After the Civil War Gould allied with James Fisk to win control of the Erie Railroad, which they used to challenge Cornelius Vanderbilt's New York Central Railroad in a battle for New York's flourishing freight trade. Both sides indulged in an orgy of bribery, stock market fraud, and judicial injunctions as they competed to dominate rail service in the Hudson River Valley. Gould, Fisk, and Vanderbilt became entrenched in a power struggle that compromised railroad service in New York and directly challenged the viability of the Eastern financial community.

In an attempt to corner the nation's gold supply in 1869, Gould caused a financial uproar among commodities investors and the nation's banks, as Wall Street experienced its first "Black Friday." Gould and Fisk earned many enemies with their cutthroat tactics, and Fisk was mysteriously murdered in 1872. After liquidating his principal shares of stock in the Erie Railroad, Gould quickly resigned as president of the Erie and left it in financial chaos.

Gould used his Erie assets to capture temporary control of the Union Pacific Railroad in 1873. Later in opposition to the same company he helped to build, Gould tried to stop its growth by buying the rival railroads that encircled Union Pacific's tracks. He was an unabashed opportunist, and his ruthless takeover tactics ruined many regional railroads.

Gould built a large railroad network in the Southwest and allied himself with the Southern Pacific Railroad in an attempt to destroy the Atchison, Topeka, and Santa Fe. He fought ruinous, undercutting rate wars, paid out dividends that were unearned, and created panics and rumors to get rid of rivals or to unload worthless stock on the market.

During his infamous career, Gould influenced the destiny of every major railroad in the United States, and by 1890 he reputedly owned over half the railroad mileage in the Southwest. He also owned most of New York's elevated lines and had controlling interest in the Western Union Company. A chagrined financial writer on Wall Street candidly summarized his selfish impact on the course of American railroads: "His touch is death."

The official photographer for the Atchison, Topeka and Santa Fe Railroad lived in this home that is detailed with mythological creatures along its facade.

market collapsed, speculators liquidated their dwindling assets and left Topeka for new opportunities elsewhere. By 1895 the town's population had dropped by five thousand.

As consumers left Topeka many local businesses failed, forcing their owners into bankruptcy. Bank notes went unpaid, and Topeka financial institutions absorbed tremendous losses on under-collateralized loans. Even the Santa Fe Railroad, which had invested heavily in the Topeka real estate market to finance its development of a transcontinental railroad line, found itself drastically overextended; it too fell into receivership in 1895.

Those residents who remained in Topeka were not the speculators and entrepreneurs who had come and gone with the real estate boom. They were responsible settlers looking for a peaceful community in which to raise their families. Faced with a troubled local economy, Topekans in the 1890s sought social and religious support to sustain their survival. Labor unions, civic improvement groups, and volunteer service organizations proliferated.

Schools and churches were built primarily by community volunteer efforts, and the welfare of minorities, immigrants, and children became very important issues for civic discussion. Temperance and Suffrage movements enlisted local support from church and social memberships. The

Beginning in 1830 with the appearance of Peter Cooper's "Tom Thumb" steam engine, railroads began to proliferate across America. Train travel gained quick acceptance as rail lines were laid between most major cities in the Northeast. During the next several decades over thirty thousand miles of new track interlinked the eastern United States. Port cities such as Boston and New York flourished as ships and trains exchanged their cargoes, while passenger cars carried travelers along the Atlantic seaboard between Philadelphia and Charleston by way of a seven-hundred-mile coastal express line.

By 1850 rail construction had established train routes throughout the South and Midwest. Railroad networks joined New Orleans and the Gulf of Mexico ports with Chicago and The Great Lakes waterways. Southern and Northern ports competed for lucrative connections to the Western frontier. Before the Civil War, rival cities located on the Mississippi River, such as Memphis and St. Louis, vied for control of riverboat and railroad activity, to become the hub of transcontinental trade .

The Civil War destroyed many of the South's tracks, and most commerce between the East Coast and inland cities shifted to the intact network of Northeast canals and rail lines. Midwestern cities such as Chicago, St. Louis, and Topeka became important transportation centers for westward expansion; track was laid at the rate of over four thousand miles a year after the war. Eventually over two hundred fifty thousand miles of rail lines, one-third of the world's total, crisscrossed the American continent.

The first transcontinental line was chartered by Congress in 1862 with the passage of the Pacific Railway Act, which authorized the Union Pacific to build westward from Nebraska and the Central Pacific to work eastward from Sacramento. The two construction crews raced towards each other to meet at Promontory Point, Utah, where their efforts were joined by a symbolic golden spike on May 10, 1869. Their combined seventeen hundred miles of track brought the Atlantic and Pacific coasts within a week's travel of each other.

To subsidize the building of this epic railroad line across the nation, the federal government donated a continuous strip of public land ten miles wide on either side of the proposed route. It also provided for incentive loans ranging from sixteen thousand to forty-eight thousand dollars for each mile of track completed. Public grants to build similar projects eventually gave the railroads more than one hundred thirty million acres of land and sixty-four million dollars in federal loans.

During the second half of the nineteenth-century Congress chartered most of the major railroad companies in the United States. As a result, the Northern Pacific Railroad linked the Pacific Northwest territory with the Great Lakes region. The Atlantic & Pacific Railroad was merged into the well-known Atchison, Topeka & Santa Fe, which created another national route in 1881 that extended across New Mexico and Arizona to California.

These transcontinental railroad lines were a great engineering feat, but they were produced in a scurrilous fashion. Political corruption and financial greed infiltrated construction schemes based on public land grants and generous government loans. The rival railroads hastily built lines to get more land; bridges and tracks were weak, and accidents were frequent. The Union Pacific and Central Pacific crews even engaged in open warfare with each other. This wild scramble for land and money led to the construction of unnecessary projects fueled by risky financial speculation.

In many ways the railroads in America symbolized the ambition and determination that carried the United States towards its self-proclaimed Manifest Destiny of expansionism in the nineteenth-century. As ribbons of steel stretched westward across the frontier territories, optimistic settlers followed these tracks to establish new communities and trade centers. The steam locomotives that opened the wilderness to civilization and progress manifested the power and drive of the American dream.

Traditional steam locomotives like this Colorado coal burner once carried passengers and freight across the United States. Topeka was a train town. It served as the transportation juncture for the Union Pacific and Atchison, Topeka & Santa Fe Railroads. Many residents of Potwin Place were employed by the railroads and as the country expanded westward the trains that passed through Topeka played a vital role in the settlement of the Western frontier. There is a special collection of artifacts for train enthusiasts, including a fully restored steam locomotive with vintage passenger, main and dining cars, at the train exhibit inside Topeka's Kansas Museum of History.

*Left: **Built in 1887, this home was the residence of John A. Murray, a brilliant Topeka lawyer, who was the Chief Attorney for the State Temperance Union and later authored Murray's Prohibition Law.***

*Right: **Teetotallers only were invited to this door, as Mr. Murray became committed to providing beverages other than alcohol for the people of Kansas. He developed a coffee plantation in Mexico that he called Nueva Topeka, and Murray presided as president and general manager over this personal enterprise for abstinence.***

citizens of Topeka gained a new reputation for their moral responsibility and humanism.

By the turn of the century, the attitude and perseverance of Topeka's citizenry had stabilized the economy. Investor confidence returned, and new businesses, backed by conservative financial support, opened their doors to loyal local customers. Many of these enterprises were small family-owned operations, financed by nest eggs from relatives. Steadily, these humble storefront businesses grew into respectable corporations, and Topeka enjoyed a steady economic climb into the twentieth-century.

Topeka has maintained a stable financial equilibrium since 1900. It never become a major metropolis, since it has traditionally discouraged unbridled outside investors with little concern for community welfare. Instead, Topeka remains a friendly town, where civic pride, family tradition, and conservative values are prevalent.

Along with its hometown character, Topeka continues to function as the state capital and maintains a balanced economic, academic and cultural role. The Menniger Clinic in West Topeka and the University of Kansas in nearby Lawrence bring significant educational contributions and research activity to the larger metropolitan area. The Topeka Museum of History exhibits a fascinating collection of artifacts, documents, and memorabilia illustrating

Left: **This was the first of five homes constructed in Potwin Place built by building contractor Martin Gobrect. The Gobrects and their daughters, Alma, Eva and Fanny, occupied this house for just a few years until early 1890, while Mr. Gobrect built his family a large home nearby.**

Right: **Framing leaded, decorative windows and textured rows of brightly-colored shingles became a popular design motif for Victorian homeowners in the Midwest.**

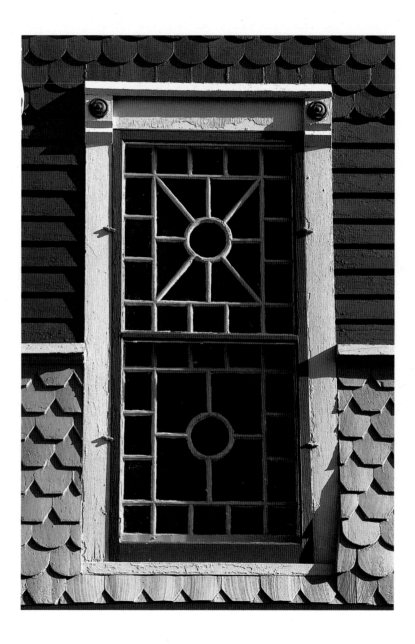

the historical evolution of Kansas.

At the heart of Topeka's heritage today is Potwin Place, which has been preserved by its proud residents as a historical landmark district. The nineteenth-century Victorians and cobblestone streets sustain the vintage atmosphere of another era, and special neighborhood events and historical home tours are conducted each year. The circular island parks and expansive elm trees insulate the quiet community from modern distractions.

In nearby Ward-Mead Park, five and one-half acres of living history include a restored 1870 Victorian Mansion, wood cabin, train depot, one-room schoolhouse, and Botanical Gardens. It is easy to imagine the stories these buildings could tell, about the Topekans who resolutely struggled to survive against environmental and economic adversities. It is a testament to their success that the trains, which traditionally brought them here, still come to Topeka, the "Railroad Rendezvous."

Left: **Potwin Place became a showplace for local architects to display new design combinations of materials and paint for their clients, many of who were newlyweds. These interpretations evolved into "fishscale" patterns that used layers of scalloped, painted shingles to create colorful textures on exterior walls.**

Right: **This home was constructed for Kansas clothier Louis Wolfe in 1886, and it was completed just in time for his new bride, Winifred Clark. She was the daughter of a Topeka judge, and the local newspaper endorsed her as an excellent catch: "The bride, daughter of one of the most prominent and highly respected citizens of Topeka, is an excellent young lady and during her long residence in this city, has acquired a countless number of friends."**

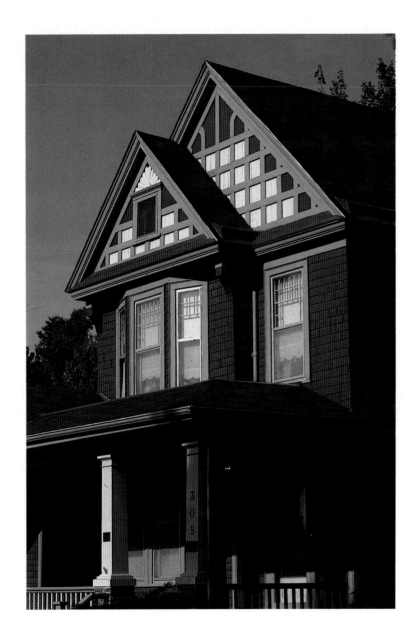

The Court House Building, constructed in the early 1890s during the peak of the silver boom in Aspen, represented the arrival of formalized justice to what had been a lawless mining camp a few years earlier.

GEORGETOWN & ASPEN

Colorado's Treasures

Right: The Georgetown Volunteer Fire Department was originally composed of four companies of firemen, each with its own engine and equipment house. The Old Missouri Firehouse, built in 1879, was the home of the Georgetown Fire Company Number One. This structure was enlarged in 1881 to include a second story and a bell tower. The historic wood buildings of Georgetown owe their survival to the vigilant volunteers who protected the town against fire damage.

During the first half of the nineteenth-century the mountains of Colorado remained mostly unsettled by pioneers, who bypassed the rugged valleys and craggy peaks of the Rockies en route to the California gold rush. As the forty-niner population in the Sierra Nevadas soared to almost four hundred thousand in little over a decade, many prospectors returned from California to try their luck in the Rockies. At the same time, the financial panic of 1857 left many unemployed workers in the East, as well as impoverished farmers in the Midwest; these destitute men eagerly headed to Colorado in search of gold and silver opportunities.

As news of the Colorado bonanza spread westward to California, an experienced group of forty-niners replaced the first wave of dilettantes in the Rockies. In 1859, a prospector named William Parsons perceptively described the impact of mining

in the mountains on American expansion: "As the discovery of gold in the mountains of California was the forerunner of an immense emigration, and the immediate cause of the erection of a new and powerful state upon the Pacific coast, so the recent discovery of the precious metal in and around the vast 'mother range' of our mountain system, is destined to exert an incalculable influence upon the growth and prosperity of the country. The Atlantic and Pacific coasts, instead of being, as they are now, divided countries, will become parts of a compact whole, joined and cemented together by bonds of mutual interest."

In his prophetic statement, Parsons anticipated the course of American expansion for the next fifty years. During the latter half of the nineteenth-century, the Western interior was subjected to a two-pronged assault, with the seasoned miners coming from the West and supplying experience and advice to the neophyte legions transplanted from the East. Optimistic explorers, prospectors, and miners crisscrossed the continent's mountain ranges from Canada to Mexico to fathom the fortunes of North America.

Colorado was at the heart of this quest for prosperity. In just a few months, Denver grew from a territory town of twenty cabins to a tent city of thousands of temporary shelters along Cherry Creek. Denver served

This ornately designed privy stands between the main house and the stables. Constructed with separate entrances for the Hamill family and their servants, this outhouse, according to researchers, became the secret repository for broken dishes that were coyly discarded by embarrassed kitchen workers.

*Right: **The Hamill house reflects the height of prosperity achieved during Georgetown's mining era. Mr. Hamill purchased the home from his brother-in-law in 1874 with profits gained through silver speculation. His success also enabled him to expand and improve the property surrounding the house.***

as a supply city for new mining towns that materialized around each new promising mineral strike: Central City, Cripple Creek, Georgetown, Leadville, Silver Plume, and Aspen. Each town followed a predictable pattern of rapid growth, ad hoc self-government, and gradual demise when the richest claims had panned out.

Whenever the rush for gold or silver triggered this cycle, each boom town in the Rockies underwent accelerated phases of fame and fortune. When a new town mushroomed around a prodigious strike, an honor code among miners generally respected each other's original claims. If claim trading and selling obscured matters of ownership, town meetings were held to appoint local officials, who acted as arbitrators to resolve disputes. A tradition of grassroots democracy maintained civic order, and a credo of fairness to all miners usually prevailed over selfish frontier violence.

Most mining camps did not survive long enough, however, to become permanent towns. Too soon the precious metal that attracted residents began to dwindle, and the transient population of miners would move on to the next promising strike. Countless temporary settlements in the mountains, with no long-term source of income, faded into oblivion as mining ghost towns. Communities in the Rockies that experienced rapid prosperity from mining were short-lived, and the typical boom-to-bust cycle often lasted less than a decade.

Seven years after George Jackson's discovery of gold at Clear Creek, miners had established over six hundred mining districts in Colorado. Historians estimate that by 1900, perhaps as many as one hundred thousand mining sites spanned the Western frontier. Most of these locations were little more than excavations, diggings, and mine shafts. Some of these strikes sustained enough wealth to provide their owners with personal fortunes, which they often used to build elegant Victorian residences for comfortably enjoying their early retirement.

Two brothers, George and David Griffith, exemplified the personal success that many Colorado transplants achieved through their mining. As farmers migrating from Bourbon County, Kentucky, the Griffith brothers arrived too late to capitalize on initial discoveries at Central City and Idaho Springs. The Griffiths pushed farther west along the main branch of Clear Creek, where they discovered gold at the confluence of two streams. They staked their claim, established the Griffith Mining District, and named a small cluster of newly-built cabins on the site, "George Town."

Although Georgetown did not produce large amounts of gold, silver was abundant, and the area prospered from the silver boom

Constructed in 1900 near the close of the silver mining era, this home reflects the growing popularity of Queen Anne style at the turn of the century. Variegated ornamental shingles on the gable were often used for decoration on houses built in the late Victorian Era.

GEORGE JACKSON

On January 6, 1859, a frustrated, freezing prospector named George Jackson chanced upon some mineral hot springs in the snowy Rockies about thirty miles west of Denver. After building a bonfire to thaw a sandbar along the south fork of Clear Creek, Jackson scraped some slushy gravel into his tin cup. He then carefully rinsed away the light sand as he had learned to do from several years of placer mining in California. As he had hoped, a few heavy yellow flakes and a tiny gold nugget glistened unmistakably in the water.

Jackson concealed his discovery, marked his location on a tall fir tree standing a discreet distance from the sandbar, and headed for Denver to stake his claim. Later he wrote in his diary, "I went to bed and dreamed of riches galore in that bar. If I only had a pick and pan instead of a hunting knife and the cup, I could dig out a sack full of the yellow stuff. My mind ran upon it all night long. I dreamed all sorts of things — about a fine house and good clothes, a carriage and horses, travel, what I would take to the folks in old Missouri

and everything you can think of — I had struck it rich! There were millions in it!"

Jackson returned to his stake after the spring thaw, and by May of 1859 news of his lucky strike had attracted hordes of desperate prospectors to the Pikes Peak region of the Rockies. Many of these new arrivals had already responded during the previous summer to exaggerated newspaper reports of gold traces found along the South Platte River. A *Kansas City Journal of Commerce* headline had zealously proclaimed, "THE NEW ELDORADO!!! GOLD IN KANSAS TERRITORY !!!"

Jackson's claim was no fluke, however, and in the hectic era that followed, thousands of inexperienced opportunists left their homes in the East and Midwest in covered wagons emblazoned with slogans such as, "Pike's Peak or Bust." Hundreds of mountain outposts sprang up, where naive hopefuls with little more than a pick, shovel, and pan scraped and washed the earth for surface gold. Most of these greenhorns had no practical knowledge of prospecting or mining, and many defeated novices returned home "busted."

The current owners of this home have carefully selected flowering plants in lilac and lavender hues for the grounds to complement the plum-colored exterior.

Gold was first found in Clear Creek, which flows by this Georgetown home built in 1868. The schoolteacher who originally owned this house held classes on the property until the Georgetown Public School opened in 1875.

during the next two decades. By the 1860s, new milling and smelting techniques had made silver mining very profitable, and several mills and smelters were constructed near Georgetown to crush and process the silver ore. The neighboring town of Silver Plume was established two miles up Clear Creek Canyon, and both communities profited from the plentiful silver ore deposits in the area.

Georgetown grew rapidly during the next decade, as miners came to work the lucrative silver mines. Merchants, doctors, lawyers, journalists, and saloon operators followed in the wake of the miners. By 1870, the town boasted over three thousand residents, four volunteer fire departments, various church congregations, and a public schoolhouse was under construction. Georgetown became the commercial hub and service center for the extensive mining activity in the surrounding region.

Many residents who did not personally work the silver and gold mines would "grubstake" new prospectors. They would supply an underfinanced miner with equipment and supplies in exchange for a share (usually half) of any claim their "partner" should discover. Grubstaking was very popular in the Rockies, and some investors made phenomenal profits from their sponsorship of successful miners. Probably the most famous of these vicarious wealth seekers

Left: **This house built in 1875, is the source of a ghost story told by residents. According to legend, the original owner died a mysterious, unnatural death in an upstairs bedroom, which was torn down by its superstitious second owners. Nearly one hundred years later, the present owners decided to reconstruct the room according to the original house plans. During the reconstruction of the room, inexplicable supernatural incidents haunted the construction workers; new wallpaper, for example, was shredded, as if by the hand of an invisible ghost. Apparently the "ghost" continued to cause a nuisance in the upper room until construction was completed, when the disruption finally ceased.**

Right: **This home was built in 1876 by Eli S. Streeter, a well-known local mining investor. He hoped that the large size and ornate detailing of his new home would further his status in the community. Tax records indicate that there had been a small cabin on the property before 1876, but with the construction of his new house, the value of Streeter's property soon tripled.**

was H.A.W. Tabor, a cantankerous store-keeper in Leadville. He gave a seventeen-dollar grubstake to two prospectors and, one year later had realized a profit of one million dollars from the sale of his share in the silver mine his partners operated.

The discovery of huge silver deposits in the Leadville area brought a new onslaught of wealth seekers to central Colorado, who ventured deeper into the higher elevations of the Rockies in search of untapped treasures. Prospectors ascended across the Continental Divide at Independence Pass, ignoring a federal treaty that reserved the Western Slope as Ute Indian Territory. These newcomers reached the Roaring Fork Valley in June 1879, where an encampment, called Ute City, emerged around a traditional Indian spring.

As the miners continued to fan out and stake claims near Smuggler's Mountain, their encroachment upon Indian land unleashed a violent backlash. The Utes along the White River northwest of Aspen ambushed a group of intruders and massacred eleven whites. The terrified survivors fled back to Leadville, while federal troops met with Chief Ouray to negotiate a new treaty that would allow mining of the Ute Territory.

A peaceful accommodation was reached between the Indians and the miners, who returned to Ute City under the leadership of an entrepreneur named H. B. Gillespie. It was Gillespie who organized the first town meeting and organized the local government. After purchasing a number of claims near Spar Gulch, Gillespie left Colorado for Washington, D.C., to request mail service, raise capital for mining development, and lobby for telegraph and railroad lines to the Rockies.

A rival mining promoter, B. Clark Wheeler, heard of Gillespie's plans for the area, and began selling options to Roaring Fork claims he had already purchased in Leadville. During the following winter, Wheeler snowshoed over the range to Ute City, where he discovered only thirteen weakened, undernourished miners. In unscrupulous fashion, Wheeler jumped their claims and renamed the area "Aspen" after the graceful trees that covered the steep mountain slopes.

When Gillespie learned of B. Clark Wheeler's takeover, he returned to Aspen with New York millionaire and industrialist Jerome B. Wheeler (no relation to the first Wheeler) to reclaim the isolated mining camp. Eventually the cause of Gillespie's group was legally upheld in the United States Supreme Court, but the town name of Aspen remained permanently. Jerome Wheeler used his wealth as former president of Macy's to purchase claims in Aspen's surrounding mountains, bring in mining equipment, and build a smelter to process the rich silver ore.

During the 1880s the mines of Aspen produced almost twenty percent of the nation's silver, and the valley's rapid influx of growth and wealth transformed the provincial river town into a glorious architectural display of alpine prosperity. In less than a decade, Aspen boasted a court house, hospital, several schools, three banks, six newspapers, and ten churches. The local population soared to twelve thousand, and the town's most prominent citizen sponsored construction of the opulent Wheeler Opera House and luxurious Hotel Jerome.

Aspen entered the 1890s filled with optimism; the Sherman Silver Purchase Act of 1890 authorized the Secretary of the Treasury to buy over fifty million ounces of silver annually, which comprised almost the entire domestic output of the precious metal. As the price of silver steadily fell, speculators cashed silver certificates for gold at the Federal Reserve, and the government faced a double dilemma of managing dwindling gold supplies and a glut of devalued silver. In an emergency session, Congress repealed the Sherman Act, and silver was demonetized, which caused financial panic.

The Silver Panic of 1893 ruined towns like Aspen, Silver Plume, and Georgetown, which had been primarily dependent on silver profits to sustain their economies.

The Maxwell House is an excellent example of eclectic Victorian architecture at its best. It displays a Second Empire roof, Italianate windows, Greek Revival pediments, and Queen Anne patterned shingles. Construction costs for this impressive building were financed in 1890 by a Georgetown grocer, who grubstaked a couple of local miners. When they hit a lucky strike, their grocer-partner became a rich man. The house is named after Frank Maxwell, a mining engineer who later lived in this house for over fifty years.

The railroads of the Rockies were the lifeline that sustained mining towns in Colorado. They provided an essential link for sending precious metal ores from mine to mill to smelter. In turn, the growth and wealth that mountain communities experienced depended on bringing in supplies, craftsmen, and professionals to provide for their isolated populations.

Railroads linking Denver and the East to the mining towns of the mountains were faced with challenging terrain. The ambitious Colorado Central Railroad laid narrow-gauge rails from Golden up Clear Creek Canyon to Central City and Georgetown in 1877 with intentions of reaping the mineral wealth of the central Rockies. Reaching the town of Silver Plume, located up a steep canyon six hundred thirty-eight feet higher than Georgetown, however, would require over three miles of specially designed track.

Narrow-gauge rails with three-foot spacing between the rails permitted the trains to turn tighter curves and climb steeper grades. For any locomotive to make the grade, the slope of ascent had to be reduced from six to four percent. Clear Creek Canyon narrowed above Georgetown to a rocky gorge known as Devil's Gate. Engineers therefore designed a series of curves and one grand loop where the track crossed over itself by way of a three-hundred-foot-long trestle almost one hundred feet above Clear Creek.

Initial completion of the high bridge was delayed because the contractor had installed the trestles backwards, causing the bridge to run downhill at a two percent grade rather than climbing uphill! Trains finally steamed into Silver Plume in 1884, but further rail progress above Clear Creek Valley was dubious. By the middle of the 1880s, attention had shifted to new silver discoveries in the Leadville and Aspen regions, and these lucrative mining areas became the primary objective among competing railroad magnates.

The narrow-gauge Denver and Rio Grande, and the broad-gauge Colorado Midland, started a race to reach Aspen in the 1880s. The narrow-gauge won when it arrived in Aspen on November 4, 1887, and it became Colorado's first link between the silver mines across the Rockies and the transcontinental connections through Denver. Legendary towns like Silverton, Telluride, Ouray, and Cripple Creek shipped millions of dollars worth of precious ore by way of the narrow-gauge "Silver Circuit" in the central Colorado mountains.

As the dream of extended westward commercial activity faded for the owners of the isolated railroad line between Georgetown and Silver Plume, the operators of the Georgetown Loop turned to Victorian tourists for business. The precarious route up Clear Creek Valley became known as the "famous knot in a railroad," and visitors from Denver flocked to Georgetown during summer excursions to ride the novelty line. As the decades slipped by, the Clear Creek route lost its tourist clientele and became a sleepy country railroad. In 1939 the railroad and bridge were dismantled and sold unceremoniously as scrap for four hundred fifty dollars.

In 1959 a Denver attorney, with substantial mining interests in the Clear Creek Valley was convinced by preservationist James Grafton Rogers to publicly donate one hundred acres of mining claims between Georgetown and Silver Plume, which inspired a grassroots campaign to resurrect the original railroad. The gorge between Georgetown and Silver Plume was officially designated in 1966 as a National Historic Landmark District. Rerouting of the Interstate highway on the mountainside between Georgetown and Silver Plume preserved the original railroad grade and its high bridge location, and fund raising for the reconstruction of a new narrow-gauge track was achieved in 1982. In 1984, one hundred years after completion of the original bridge, two double-headed Shay locomotives rumbled onto the rebuilt Devil's Gate High Bridge, inaugurating the second century of the Georgetown Loop.

Clear Creek Canyon narrows above Georgetown to a rocky gorge known as Devil's Gate. To reach Silver Plume by train, engineers designed a grand loop where the track crosses over itself by way of a three-hundred-foot-long trestle almost one hundred feet above Clear Creek. Initial completion of the bridge was delayed because the contractor installed the trestles backwards, causing the track to run downhill at a two percent grade rather than climbing uphill! In 1939 the railroad and bridge were dismantled and sold unceremoniously as scrap for four hundred fifty dollars. In 1982 the Boettcher Foundation granted one million dollars to build a replica of the Devil's Gate High Bridge. Today, thanks to the efforts of private foundations, public agencies, and dedicated volunteers, historical enthusiasts and railroad lovers may again leisurely travel by rail between Georgetown and Silver Plume along "the famous knot in a railroad."

Miners were notorious for their poetic sense of justice. Claim-jumping was an intolerable crime that brought severe retribution. Accused miners were quickly brought before a judge, prosecutor, and defender; all were selected from their peers. Verdicts were delivered by majority opinion, and each miner cast one vote. No time was wasted on building jails. Therefore punishment was swift, either by flogging, mutilation, or banishment from the mining camp.

Mines were shut down, smelters were closed, and eighteen hundred men in Aspen alone lost their jobs. Banks failed, businesses went bankrupt, and many residents left Colorado to resettle beyond the Rockies. When the world's largest silver nugget (weighing almost a ton) was mined in 1894 from the depths of the Smuggler Mine, the discovery was hardly mentioned in newspaper accounts.

The desperate times that plagued Colorado at the turn of the century changed the lifestyle of residents in the Rockies for decades. Places like Aspen became sleepy cowtowns, relying on ranching in the mountain valleys for economic survival. Clear Creek Canyon, however, was too rugged and steep between Georgetown and Silver Plume for ranching. The area lapsed into a haven for a few hundred eccentric holdouts and deluded prospectors, who still clung to fantasies of extracting bonanzas from the surrounding mountains.

Over a third of a century passed before a new breed of entrepreneurs discovered the potential of the Rockies. In 1936 a group of developers built a ski lodge at the confluence of Conundrum and Castle Creeks. In 1937 Andre Roch engineered the first ski trail, reached with a motorized towline that was operated by the newly-formed Aspen Ski Club. During World War II, the Tenth Mountain Division of the U.S. Army

Simple folk cottages, like this one built in 1888 for a maverick miner, shared Aspen's narrow valley with the ostentatious mansions of Colorado's silver barons.

commandeered the mountain trails around Leadville and Aspen for practicing alpine war maneuvers.

After the war Aspen began to commercially operate the first single and "world's longest ski lift." Chicago industrialist Walter Paepcke and his wife, Elizabeth, who were involved in the early development of the area as a ski resort, began to concentrate their efforts and resources towards making Aspen a cultural gathering place. In 1949 the Paepckes organized the Goethe Bicentennial Convocation in Aspen, and they persuaded Dr. Albert Schweitzer to attend as keynote speaker. This conference provided the foundation for the Aspen Institute for Humanistic Studies and the Aspen Music Festival.

The development of Aspen as a cultural and recreational community over recent decades has helped to generate new awareness for a town with rich architectural traditions. A Historic Preservation Ordinance, which provided for the protection of significant Victorian and mining landmarks, was adopted by the Aspen City Council in 1972. The Aspen Historical Society has also dedicated itself to defending the status of important buildings and sites related to Aspen's colorful heritage.

A concerted effort among private foundations, public agencies, and dedicated volunteers acted to preserve the historical

Left: **Four bricks thick, the walls of this well-proportioned Queen Anne home were made to stand for generations. Cast-iron cresting along the roof line and this unique bell-shaped balcony have been maintained in pristine condition for over a century.**

Right: **J.W. Atkinson, who built this immutable home during the 1890s was part-owner of the profitable Little Annie Mine. Known as "Three Fingered Jack," Atkinson kept law and order in Pitkin County as Aspen's Sheriff in the 1880s. His brother, who owned the local brick yard supplied the thousands of bricks used in the construction of this home.**

Left: **This recently restored house was originally built in 1886, and it is an excellent example of a traditional house that possesses more structural integrity than many contemporary buildings. With the renewed interest in Victorian architecture, new "Victorian" homes can be found in Aspen and many other historically aware communities in the United States.**

Right: **Built in 1891, this house was the residence of the local Methodist pastor. By 1892, Aspen had ten churches for its booming population of nearly ten thousand residents. Some of the remote mining towns were ministered by circuit riders, who would conduct services in tents and private homes if a church had not been established in the area.**

As Aspen's silver ore production soared around 1889, the commercial district of town acquired an architectural affluence that is still evident by the surviving buildings that were built over a hundred years ago.

legacies of the Clear Creek Valley as well. In the 1960s a proposed freeway through the original site of Georgetown threatened to demolish over two hundred vintage Victorians. Preservationists lobbied to have the area including Georgetown and Silver Plume protected by the U.S. Department of Interior, and in 1966 the Clear Creek Valley was officially designated as a National Historic Landmark District.

Today Georgetown and Silver Plume are bypassed by the Interstate, and visitors can still casually ride steam trains along the famous Georgetown Loop, which has linked the two mining towns for over a century. The traditional atmosphere of Georgetown as well as the historical enchantment of Aspen now attract a new generation of enthusiasts. They come to the Rockies to experience an unmistakable mountain atmosphere that invites each visitor to discover their own "Colorado Treasures."

Right: **This Aspen vignette typifies the community's oldest and most stylish neighborhood, which was once known as Bullion Row. Today this street is still lined with elegant Victorian mansions, where Aspen's wealthiest silver barons raised their families in sophisticated elegance with the unfathomable profits generated by their mountain mines.**

GEORGETOWN & ASPEN, *Colorado's Treasures*

SAN FRANCISCO

Gilded Gateway

THE VICTORIAN EXPRESS

SAN FRANCISCO
CALIFORNIA
ALL ABOARD EXCURSION

TRAIN NO.	CAR	TICKET NO.	RES. NO.
91	FIRST CLASS	011	288

PASSENGER RECEIPT

DESTINATION

This view of Alamo Square's Victorian row houses against the San Francisco modern skyline almost brings the nineteenth- and twentieth-centuries together. During the earthquake in 1906, terrified residents huddled along the slopes of this park and watched their city burn from the waterfront almost up to these houses.

San Francisco epitomized the Victorian Era. With the discovery of gold and silver in the Sierra mountains, the "city by the bay" was quickly elevated to international significance by the ambitious efforts of mining millionaires, trade barons, and railroad magnates. During the second half of the nineteenth-century, San Francisco achieved world-class status as the premier center in the American West for trade, commerce, and investment.

Sir Francis Drake, a pirate and explorer sanctioned by English royalty first landed on the shores of Northern California in 1579. For several years, Drake's ships had plundered Spanish ships and settlements along the coast of South America. By the time his sailors reached the shelter of what is now called Drake's Bay in Marin County, his fleet had been reduced to one vessel, which was crowded, overloaded, and in desperate need of repairs.

Drake and his crew spent six weeks recuperating on the Northern California coast, which they claimed for Queen Elizabeth as "Nova Albion." Drake's claim may have been precluded by a Spanish expedition in 1542, led by Juan Cabrillo; while exploring the Baja Peninsula thirty years earlier, Cabrillo had presumptuously claimed all land north of Mexico as "Alta California" for the Spanish Crown. After Drake's ship was rendered seaworthy, *The Golden Hind* continued westward across the Pacific Ocean to circumnavigate the world, leaving California unsettled.

During the next two hundred years, the Spanish continued to advance along the coastal regions of South America, Central America, and Mexico. By the 1760s the Franciscan missionaries, led by Father Junipero Serra, began their spiritual pilgrimage northward from Mexico to convert the native Indians of Alta California to Christianity. In

Flourishes and faces frequently grace the designs of both San Francisco's simple and more grandiose Victorians.

1776 a permanent outpost of several hundred Spanish soldiers was established on the future site for a presidio overlooking the entrance to San Francisco Bay.

Spain's control over Mexico and the Baja Peninsula began to weaken, however, as Mexican nationalists sought autonomy from the control of a European monarchy. In 1824 Mexico declared its independence as a republic, and the newly installed government issued generous land grants to settlers willing to populate the northern regions of Alta California. Within a decade of Mexican sovereignty, a profitable hide-and-tallow trade had developed between immigrant ranchers and Mexican shippers in the San Francisco Bay Area.

During the 1830s a peaceful bayside village called "Yerba Buena" emerged as a trading place for Indians, Mexicans, Spanish, Dutch, and even a few Kanakas from the Sandwich Isles, later known as Hawaii. American frontiersmen such as Jedediah Smith, Captain John C. Fremont, and Kit Carson blazed trails over the Sierra Nevadas that opened the prospect for Yankee migration from the East. Alta California, with its fertile soil, pleasant climate, and coastal harbors, seemed ideal for settlement in an era when western American expansion was imminent.

In 1841 a group of pioneers trekked from Mississippi across the Western wilderness to reach the settlement at Yerba Buena six months later. As the flow of Eastern immigrants to California increased dramatically in the 1840s, the Mexican government perceived their arrival as a threat to the tenuous control that Mexico had exerted over Alta California. Restrictive laws were enacted under General Vallejo's provincial authority to curtail trading practices that might challenge established Mexican interests.

The settlers that came to California in search of financial opportunity and personal freedom were not amenable to economic subjugation and autocracy, however, and a rebellious attitude towards Mexico emerged among Californians. As Texas had broken away from Mexican control in 1836, the United States hoped to extract additional territory to fulfill its Manifest Destiny of western expansion towards the Pacific Coast. Military skirmishes broke out between Mexicans and Americans in California over the region's contested future as a Mexican

Right: Bay windows have become synonymous with the architecture of San Francisco. These prominent windows were the rage in the Bay Area during the 1870s, and they became almost obligatory after the unadorned pioneer homes of the earlier Gold Rush period. Architectural historians can usually discern the age of a San Francisco house based on the design and quality of its glass windows.

SAN FRANCISCO, *Gilded Gateway* 231

territory, independent republic, or candidate for American statehood.

The issue came to a climax on June 14, 1846, when a mob of militants stormed into General Vallejo's Sonoma estate and announced the formation of the California Republic. Over numerous brandies haplessly served by the outnumbered General, a flag was sewn together that featured a somewhat forlorn-looking grizzly bear. As the new symbol was hoisted over the Sonoma town plaza, the Bear Flag Revolt officially announced the end of Mexican control over Alta California.

Several weeks later on July 9, Yerba Buena was seized for the United States by troops from the *U.S.S. Portsmouth*, who marched ashore and raised the American flag over the town. Later that month, a shipload of two hundred thirty-eight Mormons arrived from New York after a six-month journey around Cape Horn. They had fled persecution from the Eastern religious establishment and had hoped to rendezvous with the arrival of Brigham Young and his Latter-Day-Saints movement on the West Coast.

Young, however, had led his main group of followers westward by land only as far as the Great Salt Lake, which left the Mormon passengers of the *S.S. Brooklyn* lost in the fog of San Francisco Bay. Nevertheless, this group of salvationists attempted to rescue the souls of the relatively heathen hustlers, vagabonds, eccentrics, and hedonists that inhabited Yerba Buena. In a misguided attempt at teaching through example, their Mormon "elder," twenty-six-year-old Samuel Brannan, strutted about the town dressed in elegant suits and beaver-pelt hats, to the amusement of the rustic locals.

Brannan became an embarrassment to his fellow Mormons, who saw him more as a self-indulgent sham than as an exemplary keeper of the faith. Like a precursor to modern-day religious evangelists, he was arrested by his congregation for misuse of church funds. Brannan successfully acquitted himself with an eloquent defense that loftily stated, "Go tell Brigham Young that I'll give up the money when he sends me a receipt signed by the Lord."

In 1847 the Mayor of Yerba Buena decreed that the official town name be changed to "San Francisco," since the name of its famous bay had gained more popular recognition among sailors than the more obscure "Yerba Buena." San Francisco's population was barely five hundred in 1847, but hundreds of ships entered the Golden Gate each year. Although it was a busy port, the town itself consisted only of a few hundred buildings and tents, strewn about a muddy cove at the tip of a windy, sandy, and hilly peninsula.

Everything changed radically within a

This Lilienthal-Pratt house, of Italianate design, features carved, painted, redwood columns that combine classic style with geometric accents.

few short years, however, with the discovery of gold in the Sierra Nevada mountains of California. On January 24, 1848, a mechanic named James W. Marshall, while working on a saw mill owned by John A. Sutter, in the Sierra foothills noticed gold flakes in the water sluice. News of Marshall's discovery at Sutter's Mill inspired the most sensational race for wealth in American history — the California Gold Rush!

John Sutter was both thrilled and chagrined by the significance of finding gold on his property. As a Swiss Army officer he had come to Alta California a decade earlier during Mexican occupation; after conveniently becoming a Mexican citizen, Sutter was awarded a fifty-thousand-acre land grant in the Central Valley and foothills of the territory. He ruled over his acreage like a military officer from his headquarters at "Sutter's Fort," drafting Indians for menial labor, and recruiting settlers to manage the expansive resources of his domain.

Sutter feared that the dramatic news of

Built in 1876, this house was a wedding present for the daughter of Louis Sloss, Hanna, and her husband, Ernest Lilienthal. Decades later, their son Samuel married Alice Haas, which intertwined the Haas-Lilienthal families into a local legacy that has lasted for generations.

This twenty-eight-room mansion, which was designed in 1882, was originally the home of a prominent San Francisco banker. In 1904, the second owner added San Francisco's first car garage to park his Stanley Steamer.

234

234

From the early twentieth-century until World War II, this mansion was used by wealthy White Czarists, who fled Russia during the Communist Revolution. They opened a restaurant and nightclub on the ground floor called "Dark Eyes," used the main level as a gambling hall, and kept prostitutes in the upper bedrooms.

a gold strike on his land would invoke an invasion of his estate, so he swore his workers to an oath of secrecy about the treasure buried below them. Inevitably, however, rumors raced across the country about Sutter's secret horde, when his employees curiously began exchanging gold dust for provisions in the area. Sutter's Fort was the worst place in the West to hide the obvious, since most Eastern immigrants stopped there after crossing the Sierra Nevadas to acquire supplies and information about the prospects ahead.

On March 15, the persistent rumor of Sierra gold was inauspiciously published on the back page of the territory's first newspaper, the *Californian*. A week later, an investigative reporter from San Francisco embarked on a week-long journey to Sutter's Mill to confirm the story, where he was escorted on a carefully staged tour of the area by Sutter himself. The workers, who had been using every free moment to pan for gold, were shown busily working on a lumber mill. Sutter claimed that he would utilize the nearby south fork of the American River to float Sierra timber downstream, not for sluice mining. The gullible journalist returned to San Francisco, convinced by Sutter (for the time being) that the gold rumors were false.

As hard evidence of the precious metal began to trickle into San Francisco the con-spiracy of silence was finally broken by Sam Brannan. Brannan, who operated a supply store at Sutter's Fort, had reportedly purchased a huge inventory of mining equipment to stock his store, before his public announcement. On May 12, he paraded down Montgomery Street holding a large vial of gold dust and proclaimed to the citizens of San Francisco, "GOLD! GOLD! GOLD on the American River!"

Gold fever ran rampant among the townspeople, who deserted their livelihoods in San Francisco to join the assault for Sierra gold. Merchants quickly sold out of picks, shovels, food, clothes, canvas, lanterns — anything the gold-seekers thought they might need. Previously ordered goods piled up at Yerba Buena Cove, since no one remained to claim or deliver the cargo.

Within a few days, word had spread up and down California to the residents of other mission towns, who joined in the mad scramble for the mountains. As frantic orders for more mining supplies reached other parts of the country and the world new shock waves of frenzy and greed enticed countless legions of opportunists to California. As one observer surmised, "Gold fever swept the Atlantic Seaboard, jarred staid New England, coursed through the Ohio Valley and up and down the Mississippi — spread to Canada, jumped the Atlantic to England,

MINER'S TEN COMMANDMENTS

The forty-niners in the Sierras developed their own code of honor for survival during the California Gold Rush. This credo was generally accepted throughout the camps, and it became widely known as the "Miner's Ten Commandments." In 1853 these tenets of mountain justice were enacted into federal law. Here is a summarized version of those laws:

1 Thou shalt work only thy own claim.

2 Thou shalt not make any false claims, nor jump other claims. If thou do, thou must go prospecting and hire thy body out to make board and save thy bacon.

3 Thou shalt not go prospecting before thy claim gives out, nor shall thou take thy gold to the gaming table in vain.

4 Thou shalt remember the Sabbath. For in six days labor, thou canst work enough to wear out thy poor body in two years. And on the seventh day thou washest thy dirty socks, and boil thy pork and beans.

5 Thou shalt not think more of thy gold than how thou canst make it fastest and how thou wilt enjoy spending it.

6 Thou shalt not kill thy body by working in the rain. Nor destroy thyself by getting "three sheets in the wind or high seas over" while thou are swallowing down thy gold purse.

7 Thou shalt not grow discouraged nor think of going home before thou hast made thy pile, for thou knowest thou might strike a lead and keep thy manly self respect.

8 Thou shalt not steal a pick, a shovel, or a pan from thy fellow miners, nor borrow a claim, nor pan out gold from another's rifle box. For they will hang thee, or brand thee like a horse thief with the letter "R" upon thy cheek.

9 Thou shalt not tell any false tales about "good diggings" in the mountains, lest your neighbors return with naught but guns in hand and present thee with bullets, as thou shalt fall down and die.

10 Thou shall not commit unsuitable matrimony, nor neglect thy first love. If thy heart be free, thou shalt "pop the question" like a man, lest another more manly than thou step in before thee, and leave your lot to be that of a poor, despised, comfortless bachelor.

Many of San Francisco's residential lots were long and narrow, which forced an architectural emphasis on vertical styling. The primary facade was designed and decorated with careful attention to detail and proportion, while the less visible exterior walls were left relatively plain. The exception to this approach were corner lots, where elegant embellishment continued on the exposed elevations.

236

SAN FRANCISCO, *Gilded Gateway*

The tasteful decoration of this carved chimney, with its urn-and-floral motif, perfectly suits the mood of its design. Subtle pastels were selected to accentuate details, which balance the overall palette of the exterior and provide just the right amount of attention without overpowering the architecture of the house.

invaded the European continent, and stirred France and Germany, the Baltic peoples, and the Mediterranean."

Even President Polk acknowledged that the country was consumed by an unprecedented mineral mania, when he stated on December 2: "The accounts of gold are of such an extraordinary character as would scarcely command belief were it not corroborated by the authentic reports of officers in the public service who visited the mineral district and derived the facts that they detail from personal observation." Nobody seemed immune to the rash symptoms of gold fever; farmers, clerks, students, teachers, shopkeepers, artisans, soldiers, and businessmen all abandoned their vocations to become California prospectors. Like no other phenomenon in American history, the California Gold Rush affected all segments of our country's population and culture.

The first group to arrive in the gold fields were the pioneer farmers and settlers, who had originally come to California to homestead the land. They found such an abundance of gold in the virgin Sierra foothills that one ex-farmer from Illinois wrote to his friends in the Midwest, "We in this country live and move on beds of the richest minerals. We are in our infancy in wealth. It is but dawning so far as mines and rich ores are concerned. We have them for

The use of gold leaf on the details of many San Francisco houses has become a popular way to let these designs sparkle in the sunlight.

When urban expansion (or disaster) created a new neighborhood in San Francisco, the most popular style of the season usually prevailed upon the rows of new buildings that soon appeared. Each historic district in this city tends to have its own concentration of signature style residences. This picturesque Queen Anne home represents the last phase of Victorian styles in San Francisco, and it illustrates the return to gabled roofs.

LOTTA CRABTREE

Lotta Crabtree personified the spirit of the California Gold Rush. As a child, she was brought to the West Coast by her father, John, a bookseller, and her mother, Mary Ann, who were among the thousands of transplanted settlers consumed by "gold fever" during the early 1850s. The Crabtrees arrived in San Francisco at the peak of the city's theatrical craze, where tiny Lotta was taught to dance and sing by a popular entertainer named Lola Montez.

In 1855 Lotta made her stage debut at the age of eight at Rabbit Creek, a remote mining camp in the Sierras, where her mother placed her on the stage of a noisy hall filled with rowdy miners. Lotta bravely sang and danced for the boisterous crowd, which showered her performance with gold nuggets. That year, Lotta and her mother joined a troupe of traveling performers, who toured the Sierra mountain circuit with a caravan of mules and wagons.

As Lotta performed in the mountains over the next few years, her reputation grew and eventually she returned to San Francisco to perform regular engagements in the city's variety halls. Her appearance was striking, with flaming red hair and sparkling black eyes, and her diminutive figure gave her intricate dance steps a magical innocence that she carried into adulthood. As a young woman, Lotta's act became more risqué as she added piquant elements of burlesque, but her childlike quality lent any controversial repertoire a saving grace.

As an adult Lotta toured America and Europe with mixed success, depending on the abilities of the local promoter. She missed the loyalty of her regular fans in San Francisco, where she returned to perform until 1891. Upon retirement in her favorite city, Lotta donated a twenty-four-foot-high monument, which still stands at the intersection of Market and Kearny Streets.

Lotta chose to live out her life in San Francisco as a secluded woman. Contrary to her public image as an outgoing performer, she was a very private person off-stage, and she had few close personal relationships during her lifetime. Her closest companion was her mother, who had guided Lotta's career and managed her finances astutely. Lotta died a rich woman, but, with no immediate family or surviving heirs to claim her estate, her personal fortune, earned principally before San Francisco audiences, was bequeathed to local children's charities.

The bold floral design in this brightly painted pediment covers a favorite wooden material used by the carpenter who built this house. During the Victorian Era, redwood was available in abundance and it was easy to carve into complex shapes and figures. Many of San Francisco's houses still stand due to the endurance of redwood and its resilient ability to resist the elements.

SAN FRANCISCO, *Gilded Gateway* 241

picking up." As these initial Californians were quickly joined by thousands of forty-niners from other states, hundreds of temporary mining camps sprang up along the western foothills of the Sierra Nevadas.

Between 1849 and the early 1850s, crazed prospectors recklessly scoured the landscape in search of gold veins. Each time a strike was made, a boomtown was born overnight, with names like Murderer's Bar, Drytown, Slumgullion, Freezeout, and Humbug. Over five hundred such colorful spots were dismantled as quickly as they were built, when the local supply of gold was exhausted. Many addicted miners spent most of their lives scraping and squandering gold, in an endless cycle of "boom-to-bust" experiences.

The majority of gold discoveries along the Sierra foothills were located within a relatively narrow corridor. Most prospectors believed that they had tapped into one continuous Mother Lode, which ranged in width from a few miles to several hundred yards. In fact, geological evidence suggests that California gold was first exposed along the surface of scattered fissures in the Sierra Nevada. These deposits were gradually eroded by white water rivers, and most of the surface gold was eventually distributed downstream along riverbeds in the foothills. The forty-niners readily collected these gold deposits through a simple panning technique that used water to separate the heavier gold

A fire in 1988 destroyed much of this house, which was initially built at the turn of the century. After the fire, the house was restored to its former grandeur, with authentic brass fittings, period chandeliers, and exact replicas of all doors, moldings, and vintage details.

Right: This home survived both the 1906 and 1989 earthquakes in excellent condition, with only a few hairline cracks in evidence. Wood was the favored material in San Francisco, because of its availability, value, and relative safety during earthquakes. Brick or stone breaks into lethal fragments during a quake, while a frame house holds together; although they might settle, tilt, or burn in the aftermath, wood houses did not readily crumble during earthquakes.

flakes and nuggets from scoops of sand.

After the riverbeds were panned out, mining operations in the Sierras became more mechanized with the use of sluice boxes, followed by high-pressure hydraulic strip-mining. These techniques, though initially more capital-intensive, yielded the majority of gold that ultimately was mined in California. Profits soared to record levels each year during the Gold Rush. The yield increased from ten million dollars in 1849 to a total of over a half-billion dollars in less than a decade, making the Mother Lode of the Sierras the richest mining region in the world during the 1850s.

Most of the cargo destined for the Sierra foothills passed through San Francisco, which underwent dramatic changes as a result. To create temporary wharfage for the hundreds of arriving passenger and cargo ships, the shallow Yerba Buena Cove was filled in with "conglomerate layers of cook stoves, tobacco crates, flour bags, barrels of spoiled beef, rolls of sheet lead, washing machines, discarded clothing, and a slight covering of earth." Many deserted ships drifting in the harbor were converted into hotels, stores, and jails, or simply towed near shore and sunk for landfill.

San Francisco was so isolated from its suppliers in the 1850s, that the demand for a particular item could not be accurately

The musical instruments depicted in this gold embellishment represent the glorious era when this mansion was filled with music, art, and culture. This opulent Victorian was the residence of Madame Kreling, the proprietress of the Tivoli Opera House. The building's artistic legacy continued when it became the Yiddish Cultural Center, which harbored Russian artists and performers who fled after the Communist Revolution.

Right: **This twenty-two-room mansion was originally designed and built in 1892 for Oregon lumber baron D.B. Jackson, who lived here with his wife until 1898. The second owner, Mrs. Ernestine Kreling, was the widow of two Kreling brothers, first Joseph and then William. The Yiddish Cultural Center offered support to Jewish artists and performers here until 1961. Relegated to exist as a rooming house until 1975, the neglected mansion finally succumbed to a decade of "communal activities." In 1985, the current owners embarked on an extensive process of restoration to return this Victorian classic to its original grandeur; now, called Chateau Tivoli, it is offered as an exclusive facility for special events.**

SAN FRANCISCO, *Gilded Gateway*

anticipated, and merchants on the East Coast resorted to speculation. They simply loaded ships with cargo they hoped would sell profitably upon its arrival several months later in San Francisco. If the goods were scarce, the merchant commanded a high price at pierside auctions and became rich. On the other hand, if there was a temporary glut of a certain product when it reached San Francisco Bay, the surplus crates might be discarded for landfill. A shrewd speculator could realize a fortune by racing out to the bay entrance and meeting the arrival of a new supply ship. Before the oblivious captain could assess the onshore price of his inventory, he would naively agree to sell his cargo below the current market value.

In 1849 San Francisco's predominantly male population grew from six thousand to thirty thousand in less than four months, although not all the new arrivals came exclusively in search of gold. The city was thronged by lustful men seeking pleasure in

Continuing this mansion's legacy of culture, the **Chateau Tivoli** *offers unique facilities for meetings, performances, and celebrations. It provides guests with the opportunity to experience musical, educational, and social events in the grand salons and parlors of this magnificently restored Victorian environment.*

all forms: food, drink, gambling, and women of ill repute. San Francisco became a decadent conglomeration of noisy eateries, smoky saloons, expensive gambling halls, and posh bordellos — what Mark Twain called "a wild, free, disorderly, grotesque society."

Crime prevailed in the rowdy streets of early San Francisco, which compelled most bawdy establishments to hire thugs for protecting their operations. The San Francisco Police were initially recruited mostly from reformed criminals, who arbitrarily meted out justice according to their personal sensibilities; if an old acquaintance was apprehended, he was probably spared the punishment reserved for less familiar miscreants. So-called "tax revenues" collected from local dens of iniquity were in actuality thinly-veiled payoffs to secure the political favor of corrupt city officials.

Despite its problems, San Francisco quickly became an international gateway city on the West Coast. Just two years after the Gold Rush began, San Francisco ranked fourth in the nation for foreign trade, after New York, Boston, and New Orleans. On September 9, 1850, California was hastily granted statehood by Congress, which extended its federal authority to the West Coast. Sutter's Fort, where several politically influential and wealthy merchants lived,

became known as Sacramento, the state capital; but it was San Francisco that captured the hearts and minds of California's aristocrats.

Many of the investors who came to San Francisco during the Gold Rush era were educated, cultured Easterners accustomed to social grace and civilized behavior. In the 1850s San Francisco boasted more college graduates than any other American city. Most of the gold produced in the Sierras found its way back to San Francisco, where mining millionaires, trade barons, and philanthropic financiers supported the cultivation of the arts in the city.

San Francisco attracted a large enclave of performers, musicians, and writers, who participated in contemporary theatrical productions, classical music recitals, and literary club readings. Because of California's geographic isolation from the rest of the United States, San Francisco transplants, many of who left behind their families, friends, and business associates, were starved for entertainment and news of the world. By 1852 at least a dozen newspapers provided information to Bay Area readers.

Not all new arrivals on the West Coast were able to adapt to the detachment they felt from their previous homes. Physically and financially drained from their migration across the Western wilderness, many settlers ended up in cold, drafty, leaky tents and shacks on the outskirts of the city. Cholera, pneumonia, and hepatitis proliferated in the unsanitary conditions that pervaded these encampments; for those unfortunate souls relegated to the city's darker side, the dream of California gold was tainted with despair.

These ramshackle parts of town, built of canvas and wood, were particularly susceptible to fires, which frequently imposed an unplanned version of "urban redevelopment." Incinerated shanty districts were often replaced by more affluent neighborhoods, as the prosperity of the Gold Rush expanded and improved the quality of residential construction in the city. San Francisco's growing club of millionaires commissioned architects to build flamboyant Victorians along the hilltop locations overlooking the city and the bay.

1853 brought the end of the Gold Rush, when gold production in the Sierras plummeted drastically. After five years of rapid population growth, immigration to California virtually ceased, causing an avalanche of economic repercussions. Speculators panicked and sold their real estate investments at far below former market values. Merchants, who had previously stockpiled huge inventories, found themselves glutted with unsold merchandise. Money became tight, businesses failed, and banks closed from the consequences of

Left: **This corner tower, standing almost seventy feet high, never had an assigned function, such as an observatory; it was simply added as an elaborate architectural ornament. The tower symbolizes the Victorian philosophy of "fancy over function." Painted true to its original colors, this typical San Francisco color scheme became popular in "the cool, gray city of love," where fog swept over and blanketed hilltop Victorians.**

Right: **Now home to the Foundation for San Francisco's Architectural Heritage, the Haas-Lilienthal Home, built in 1886, was occupied by two generations of the Haas family until 1972. Alice Haas was raised here with her sister, Florine. Years later after her father passed away, Alice returned with her husband Samuel Lilienthal to her childhood home, where she spent the rest of her life. Alice was devoted to her sister Florine; they lived only three blocks apart and visited constantly. Many delightful stories about the two sisters have been published.**

unpaid loans and investments turned sour.

San Francisco's economy slumped for the rest of the decade until a startling discovery was made in the spring of 1859 on the eastern slope of the Sierras, near Lake Tahoe. Placer miners, in search of gold amidst the blue clay that oozed from the mountains, inadvertently struck a bonanza by finding another precious metal in massive quantities — silver ore. The Comstock Lode, as it was called, attracted national attention, and San Francisco returned to the forefront as the transportation and trade center for a second California mineral boom.

With the Silver Rush, San Francisco was rejuvenated with activity, as a new wave of prospectors, mining investors, and speculators came westward in search of wealth. Merchants quickly sold out of pickaxes, buckboards, and mining provisions, but the popular goldpan of the forty-niners was useless in the quest of silver, which unlike gold was not so easily retrieved from the surface of the Sierra Nevadas.

Mark Twain, who visited the Comstock region at the age of twenty-six, related a humorous preconception about silver mining in 1861: "I confess, without shame, that I expected to find masses of silver lying all about the ground. I was perfectly satisfied that I was going to gather up, in a

The current residents of this impeccable Victorian have maintained a tradition begun by its original owners, who resisted modernizing this vintage home. Improvements and modifications to the interior and exterior are still chosen with respect and sensitivity for the integrity of the original architectural detailing, a process that they aptly refer to as "historical renovation."

*Right: **Water Department records are among the few documents that did not perish in the 1906 Earthquake and Fire, and these data are frequently used to ascertain a construction date for San Francisco's older buildings. This house was probably built in 1897, when city water was first supplied to the home. Many San Francisco residences in the 1800s, however, had private wells, so this method is not always reliable.***

day or two, or at the furthest a week or two, silver enough to be satisfactorily wealthy — and so my fancy was already busy with plans for spending this money." Reaching veins of silver ore, however, which were typically nestled deep inside the Sierra mountains, required laborious tunneling and the careful construction of mine shafts.

Despite the adversity involved, over forty million dollars worth of silver was extracted from the mines around Virginia City, which was linked with San Francisco by three stagecoaches a day. Most of the wealth from the Comstock Lode was deposited in San Francisco's revitalized banks, or invested in the new Pacific Coast Stock Exchange. In the decade of the Sierra Gold and Silver Rushes, San Francisco accumulated more material wealth than New York and Boston had realized in over two hundred years.

San Francisco's renewed prosperity catalyzed efforts to construct a transcontinental railway, which supporters contended would bring a steady influx of immigrants, supplies, and capital investment to California. The major proponents for railroad construction were four ambitious Sacramento businessmen named Charles Crocker, Mark Hopkins, Collis Huntington, and Leland Stanford. They petitioned Congress to provide low-interest loans and federal land grants across the country to facilitate a coast-to-coast route.

The prospect for railroad development towards the West Coast became embroiled in partisan politics, however, as Northern Federalists and Southern Secessionists battled over the issues of slavery, state's rights, and federal funding. The Civil War postponed construction of the first cross-country railroad link until May 10, 1869, when a golden spike was driven with a silver sledge at Promontory Point, Utah, to unite the Union Pacific and Central Pacific Railroads. The federal government accomplished its goal of extending its national railroad network to California, thus removing the mineral-rich West from isolation and protecting the country's resources.

The coalition of Sacramento railroad entrepreneurs, Crocker, Hopkins, Huntington, and Stanford, realized tremendous profits from the sale of land they had shrewdly purchased adjacent to the new transcontinental railway. The four-some moved their operations to San Francisco's Nob Hill, where they competed in a mansion-building contest to see who among their wealthy group could build the most dazzling monument to his financial success. San Francisco prepared for the anticipated surge of profits it expected to command from direct, efficient access to Eastern railroad connections.

The sudden addition of newcomers to the California labor force, combined with the oversupply of Eastern merchandise in the retail marketplace, created a recession in San Francisco. Unemployment soared and prices sank, because the isolation that had sustained a high demand for workers and supplies in the West had been removed. The ease of reaching San Francisco caused the city's population to double to over three hundred thousand people in just a few decades.

As San Francisco swelled with residents, the need for an urban transportation system to cope with the hilly topography became desperately apparent. A Scotsman named Andrew Hallidie provided the steep city with the perfect solution; he devised trolleys, hoisted by a series of motorized underground cables, to replace the over-burdened horses that pulled carriages up the dangerous hills. Hallidie's "cable cars" were an instant success, and by 1890 six hundred cars pulled passengers over one hundred miles of track.

San Francisco ultimately had more than just breathtaking hill climbs to overcome. At 5:12 A.M. on April 18, 1906, the earth shook violently for what must have been the city's longest minute. Brick buildings collapsed, iron trolley tracks squirmed, and glass windows shattered in every part of town. Twenty percent of the city was

leveled by the earthquake. The worst damage occurring in the North Beach and financial districts, where Yerba Buena Cove had been hastily filled with unstable debris and covered with loose dirt during the Gold Rush.

The worst damage was not caused by the earthquake itself, however, but by the uncontrollable fire that decimated the city for the next three days. Broken gas mains, ignited by fallen lanterns, started blazes over the entire metropolitan area. Water lines from out of town, which normally carried thousands of gallons to the fire hydrants in San Francisco, were broken and left dry by the tremors. The city was defenseless against the flames.

The firestorm totally consumed four-fifths of San Francisco; only shifting winds spared the western sector, with its exquisite Victorian architecture, from complete destruction. Over five hundred victims died in the inferno, and more than twenty-eight thousand buildings, spanning five hundred city blocks, were completely lost. An estimated two hundred and fifty thousand San Franciscans were left homeless, which forced most families to seek temporary shelter in tent cities erected by civil and military forces in the city's parks and the unscathed Presidio.

The nation and the world responded to San Francisco's tragic events by donating over

This house, built at the turn of the century, has had only two owners during its ninety-year history. It represents a transition from Queen Anne to Edwardian architecture, and this metamorphosis of style continued during the English reign of Edward VII, after he succeeded Queen Victoria to the throne in 1902. Most architectural historians agree that this event symbolically marked the end of the Victorian Era, although many twentieth-century architects have borrowed freely from the styles of the 1800s in their contemporary designs.

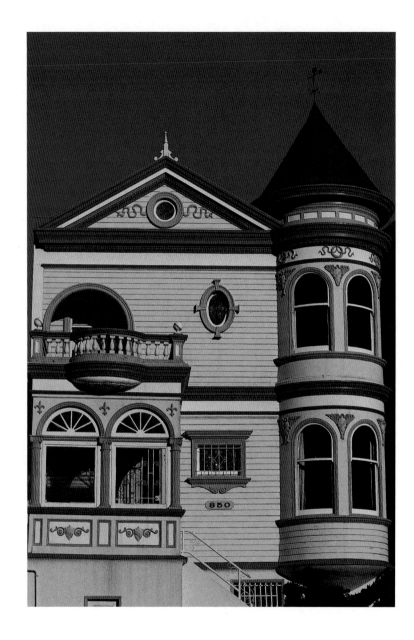

one hundred million dollars in relief funds, as well as sending countless rail and boat shipments of food, clothing, tools, and medicine. Disaster crews worked around the clock to remove smoldering debris, replace twisted trolley tracks, and reconnect water mains throughout the city. Over sixty thousand construction workers were employed to rebuild San Francisco, which emerged from its near apocalypse in 1906 to achieve even greater stature in the following years.

As the United States fulfilled its self-proclaimed destiny to become a contiguous bi-coastal nation, California became more directly influenced by national economic trends. When the New York Stock Market crashed in 1929, the Pacific Exchange self-destructed as well. As a port city dependent on maritime trade, San Francisco's shipping industry was devastated; three-out-of-four longshoremen were left jobless during America's Great Depression.

During the late 1920s ferries carried over fifty million passengers a year across San Francisco Bay. With the arrival of the automobile, however, it became clear that San Francisco, which was located on the end of a peninsula, would need a bridge system to readily handle car commuters and truck deliveries around the Bay Area. Two great bridges, the Golden Gate and the Bay Bridge, were proposed by planners to fulfill San Francisco's transportation needs.

The most difficult half of the Bay Bridge, linking San Francisco's Rincon Point to Yerba Buena Island, was completed in November 1936. At a total cost of over eighty million dollars, the bridge was supported by twin four-hundred-foot concrete towers, which required more material than was used to build the entire Empire State Building. The Golden Gate, the world's longest single suspension bridge for decades, was opened on May 27, 1937, when a quarter of a million San Franciscans walked its span in a ceremonial parade. The famous bridge, stretching over two hundred feet above the Pacific Ocean, required enough steel cable to circle the Earth three times.

San Francisco emerged from the Great Depression with two new bridges to revitalize its economy, and it celebrated with an International Exposition held on an extension of Yerba Buena Island, christened Treasure Island. As World War II approached, the island became a logistical supply center for the U.S. Navy, which transported over twenty-three million tons of war supplies through the Golden Gate. During the war, over an estimated million military personnel spent time in San Francisco, crowding the city's ornate bars and hotels with soldiers and sailors.

The wartime era was productive for San Francisco; its economy thrived on ship-building, factories, and supplying American troops stationed in the Pacific. From 1941 to 1943 the work force almost tripled, and the amount of business and industry in the Bay Area grew proportionately. Housing was at a premium, and the magnificent Victorians of the previous century were joined by mass-produced stucco houses that dotted the southern slopes of San Francisco like Spartan rows of military barracks.

Fortunately, the romanticism that originally inspired the traditional architecture of San Francisco returned in the 1960s, when architects, designers, and the city's historical preservationists began to renovate the aging Victorians that had survived the Great Earthquake and Fire of 1906. These predominantly white and homogeneous buildings were reinterpreted by the "colorist" movement; stylish owners embellished their intricate house designs with polychromatic paint schemes and consummate attention to exterior details. Some of these complex palettes combined over a dozen harmonious hues, and several San Francisco painters began to specialize in converting the hidden potential of drably painted Victorians into signed, colorful expressions of "houseart."

Thanks to the efforts of these proud homeowners, paint specialists, and historical preservation groups visitors to this unique city can enjoy outstanding examples of Victorian architecture. From the psychedelic brilliance of the 1960s to the neo-traditional gold-gilding and faux-marbling of the 1990s, Victorian architecture in San Francisco has regained popularity during recent years to reign supremely in the epitome of all Victorian cities. Ever since the Gold Rush first brought the world's attention to this magical city, San Francisco has opened itself to opportunity, imagination, and style to earn the apt title of "Gilded Gateway."

More than any other design element, stained glass epitomizes the glory of the Victorian Era. This renaissance window exemplifies the gem-like array of art glass that glitters throughout San Francisco's historical architecture.

DIRECTORY OF STREET ADDRESSES

Cover	143 M Street	Eureka, CA
p. iii	143 M Street	Eureka, CA
p. vi	Irvington-on-Hudson	Hudson, NY
p. viii	701 Louisiana Street	Lawrence, KS
p. 2	Broad Street	Nevada City, CA
p. 6	Water Street	Port Townsend, WA
p. 9	William Cody Statue	Cody, WY
p. 11	Golden Spike Monument	Promontory, UT
p. 12	207 Kingshighway	Eureka Springs, AR
p. 15	919 Elmira Road	Ithaca, NY
p. 17	506 West South Street	Kalamazoo, MI
p. 19	Irvington-on-Hudson	Hudson, NY
p. 21	1500 North Liberty Street	Independence, MO
p. 23	701 Louisiana Street	Lawrence, KS
p. 25	583 Main Street	Glen Ellyn, IL
p. 27	400 Berding Street	Ferndale, CA
p. 29	3673 West Pine Boulevard	St. Louis MO
p. 31	232 East Bleeker Street	Aspen, CO
p. 33	1041 Tennessee Street	Lawrence, KS
p. 35	216 West Ohio Street	Chicago, IL
p. 36	Cape May Point Lighthouse	Cape May, NJ
p. 37	927 Beach Avenue	Cape May, NJ
p. 38	42 Jackson Street	Cape May, NJ
p. 39	42 Jackson Street	Cape May, NJ
p. 41	1048 Washington Street	Cape May, NJ
p. 42	33 Perry Street	Cape May, NJ
p. 45	606 Columbia Avenue	Cape May, NJ
p. 46	102 Ocean Street	Cape May, NJ
p. 47	102 Ocean Street	Cape May, NJ
p. 48	645 Hughes Street	Cape May, NJ
p. 49	645 Hughes Street	Cape May, NJ
p. 51	5 Trenton Avenue	Cape May, NJ
p. 52	725 Columbia Avenue	Cape May, NJ
p. 53	725 Columbia Avenue	Cape May, NJ
p. 54	606 Columbia Street	Cape May, NJ
p. 55	725 Columbia Avenue	Cape May, NJ
p. 56	East Bay Street	Savannah, GA
p. 59	213-221 East Gaston Street	Savannah, GA
p. 61	East Bay Street	Savannah, GA
p. 63	330 Abercorn Street	Savannah, GA
p. 64	408 East Gaston Street	Savannah, GA
p. 65	410 East Huntington Street	Savannah, GA
p. 66	The Gastonian	Savannah, GA
p. 68	225 East Hall Street	Savannah, GA
p. 69	225 East Hall Street	Savannah, GA
p. 70	1921 Bull Street	Savannah, GA
p. 71	1921 Bull Street	Savannah, GA
p. 73	City Hall	Savannah, GA
p. 74	503 Whitaker Street	Savannah, GA
p. 75	Forsyth Park	Savannah, GA
p. 76	Spring Street	Eureka Springs, AR
p. 77	Spring Street	Eureka Springs, AR
p. 78	211 Spring Street	Eureka Springs, AR
p. 79	211 Spring Street	Eureka Springs, AR
p. 81	282 Spring Street	Eureka Springs, AR

p. 83	Railroad Station	Eureka Springs, AR
p. 84	256 Spring Street	Eureka Springs, AR
p. 85	256 Spring Street	Eureka Springs, AR
p. 86	158 Spring Street	Eureka Springs, AR
p. 88	44 Prospect Street	Eureka Springs, AR
p. 89	44 Prospect Street	Eureka Springs, AR
p. 91	212 Spring Street	Eureka Springs, AR
p. 92	207 Kingshighway	Eureka Springs, AR
p. 93	207 Kingshighway	Eureka Springs, AR
p. 94	Galveston Harbor	Galveston, TX
p. 96	1702 Ball Street	Galveston, TX
p. 97	1702 Ball Street	Galveston, TX
p. 98	926 Winnie Street	Galveston, TX
p. 99	926 Winnie Street	Galveston, TX
p. 100	2402 Avenue L	Galveston, TX
p. 101	2402 Avenue L	Galveston, TX
p. 103	2402 Avenue L	Galveston, TX
p. 104	2328 Broadway Avenue	Galveston, TX
p. 105	2328 Broadway Avenue	Galveston, TX
p. 107	Silk Stocking District	Galveston, TX
p. 108	1826 Sealy Avenue	Galveston, TX
p. 109	1826 Sealy Avenue	Galveston, TX
p. 110	1402 Broadway Avenue	Galveston, TX
p. 111	1402 Broadway Avenue	Galveston, TX
p. 113	Sealy and Broadway Avenues	Galveston, TX
p. 114	City Fountain Plaza	Marshall, MI
p. 116	333 North Kalamazoo Street	Marshall, MI
p. 117	333 North Kalamazoo Street	Marshall, MI
p. 118	107 North Kalamazoo Street	Marshall, MI
p. 119	107 North Kalamazoo Street	Marshall, MI
p. 121	603 North Kalamazoo Street	Marshall, MI
p. 123	218 South Eagle Street	Marshall, MI
p. 125	332 Division Street	Marshall, MI
p. 126	337 North Kalamazoo Street	Marshall, MI
p. 127	337 North Kalamazoo Street	Marshall, MI
p. 128	410 North Eagle Street	Marshall, MI
p. 129	410 North Eagle Street	Marshall, MI
p. 130	401 East Mansion Street	Marshall, MI
p. 131	401 East Mansion Street	Marshall, MI
p. 132	Bench & Washington Streets	Galena, IL
p. 133	804 Park Avenue	Galena, IL
p. 135	605 Prospect Street	Galena, IL
p. 136	513 Bouthillier Street	Galena, IL
p. 137	513 Bouthillier Street	Galena, IL
p. 139	Bench Street	Galena, IL
p. 141	Mississippi River	Hannibal, MO
p. 142	200 Park Avenue	Galena, IL
p. 143	200 Park Avenue	Galena, IL
p. 144	1008 Park Avenue	Galena, IL
p. 145	1008 Park Avenue	Galena, IL
p. 146	407 Park Avenue	Galena, IL
p. 148	Highway 20 West	Galena, IL
p. 149	310 Hill Street	Galena, IL
p. 150	Dubuque Harbor	Dubuque, IA
p. 152	1207 Grove Terrace	Dubuque, IA
p. 153	1207 Grove Terrace	Dubuque, IA
p. 154	7th and Central Streets	Dubuque, IA
p. 155	Clock Tower Square	Dubuque, IA
p. 157	504 Bluff Street	Dubuque, IA
p. 159	Fenelon Place Elevator	Dubuque, IA
p. 161	1105 Grove Terrace	Dubuque, IA
p. 163	St. Mary's Spire	Dubuque, IA
p. 164l.	1497 Central Avenue	Dubuque, IA
p. 164r.	1375 Locust Street	Dubuque, IA
p. 165	1375 Locust Street	Dubuque, IA
p. 166	1389 Locust Street	Dubuque, IA
p. 167	Clock Tower Plaza	Dubuque, IA
p. 168	Old Court House & Arch	St. Louis, MO

p. 171	2301 Lafayette Avenue	St. Louis, MO
p. 172	2006 Lafayette Avenue	St. Louis, MO
p. 173	1532 Mississippi Avenue	St. Louis, MO
p. 174	1719 Waverly Place	St. Louis, MO
p. 175	1719 Waverly Place	St. Louis, MO
p. 177	1534 Mississippi Avenue	St. Louis, MO
p. 179	1800 Kennett Place	St. Louis, MO
p. 180	2336 Whittemore Place	St. Louis, MO
p. 181	2336 Whittemore Place	St. Louis, MO
p. 182	1425 Missouri Street	St. Louis, MO
p. 183	1813 Kennett Place	St. Louis, MO
p. 184	Lafayette Square	St. Louis, MO
p. 187	1822-34 Lafayette Avenue	St. Louis, MO
p. 188	Kansas Historical Museum	Topeka, KS
p. 190	123 Greenwood Street	Topeka, KS
p. 191	123 Greenwood Street	Topeka, KS
p. 193	134 Greenwood Street	Topeka, KS
p. 194	238 Woodlawn Street	Topeka, KS
p. 195	238 Woodlawn Street	Topeka, KS
p. 197	401 Woodlawn Street	Topeka, KS
p. 199	Durango-Silverton Train	Silverton, CO
p. 200	127 Woodlawn Street	Topeka, KS
p. 201	127 Woodlawn Street	Topeka, KS
p. 202	222 Greenwood Street	Topeka, KS
p. 203	222 Greenwood Street	Topeka, KS
p. 204	303 Woodlawn Street	Topeka, KS
p. 205	305 Greenwood Street	Topeka, KS
p. 206	505 North 8th Street	Aspen, CO
p. 207	Old Missouri Firehouse	Georgetown, CO
p. 208	Argentine Street	Georgetown, CO
p. 209	Argentine Street	Georgetown, CO
p. 211	811 Rose Street	Georgetown, CO
p. 212	715 8th Street	Georgetown, CO
p. 213	715 8th Street	Georgetown, CO
p. 214	605 8th Street	Georgetown, CO
p. 215	711 Griffith Street	Georgetown, CO
p. 217	409 4th Street	Georgetown, CO
p. 219	Georgetown Loop Train	Georgetown, CO
p. 220	Brick Alley	Aspen, CO
p. 221	100 East Bleeker Street	Aspen, CO
p. 222	128 East Main Street	Aspen, CO
p. 223	128 East Main Street	Aspen, CO
p. 224	320 West Main Street	Aspen, CO
p. 225	208 East Hopkins Street	Aspen, CO
p. 226	Independence Building	Aspen, CO
p. 227	101 East Hallam Street	Aspen, CO
p. 228	Steiner Street	San Francisco, CA
p. 230	1782 Pacific Street	San Francisco, CA
p. 231	1782 Pacific Street	San Francisco, CA
p. 232	1818 California Street	San Francisco, CA
p. 233	1818 California Street	San Francisco, CA
p. 234	1198 Fulton Street	San Francisco, CA
p. 235	1198 Fulton Street	San Francisco, CA
p. 237	1834 California Street	San Francisco, CA
p. 238l.	700 Broderick Street	San Francisco, CA
p. 238r.	700 Broderick Street	San Francisco, CA
p. 239	700 Broderick Street	San Francisco, CA
p. 241	236 Ashbury Street	San Francisco, CA
p. 242	309 Steiner Street	San Francisco, CA
p. 243	309 Steiner Street	San Francisco, CA
p. 244	1057 Steiner Street	San Francisco, CA
p. 245	1057 Steiner Street	San Francisco, CA
p. 246	1057 Steiner Street	San Francisco, CA
p. 248	2007 Franklin Street	San Francisco, CA
p. 249	2007 Franklin Street	San Francisco, CA
p. 250	3100 Clay Street	San Francisco, CA
p. 251	3100 Clay Street	San Francisco, CA
p. 253	850 Steiner Street	San Francisco, CA
p. 255	850 Steiner Street	San Francisco, CA

p. 256	505 North 8th Street	Aspen, CO
p. 260	Firehouse Museum	Nevada City, CA
p. 261	232 East Bleeker Street	Aspen, CO
p. 267	463 Pacific Street	Telluride, CO
p. 268	744 Adams Street	Port Townsend, WA
p. 271	2 Gothic Street	Paris, ME
p. 272	Hyde Street	San Francisco, CA
p. 274	Iolani Palace	Honolulu, HI
p. 276	Golden Spike Monument	Promontory, UT
p. 278	Lahaina Hotel	Lahaina, HI
p. 279	The Victorian Village	Golden, CO
p. 280	143 M Street	Eureka, CA
Back Cover	North Conway Train Station	North Conway, NH

GLOSSARY

Acroterion: A pedestal or design on the ends or apex of a pediment.

Apex: The peak or tip of a pyramidal or hipped roof, or spire.

Apron: The horizontal piece of trim under the stool of a window.

Arabesque: A decorative pattern that employs foliage, flowers, fruit, human and animal figures, interlaced lines, or bands in geometrical forms.

Arch: A structural, weight-bearing or decorative curve, described in a number of differing arcs, such as: elliptical, pointed, lancet or horseshoe.

Architrave: The lower section of the classical entablature that rests on the top of columns. Part of Greek temple designs.

Art Nouveau: An art movement starting in Europe in the 1880s and 1890s with emphasis on the curved line and curved surfaces.

Astragal: Usually a small, semi-circular molding separating the necking from the shaft of a column or pilaster; also used under the egg-and-dart molding, and often cut into beads, either round or elongated.

Bague: A small molding around a column or square post, about halfway between the base and cap; sometimes more than one.

Balloon Frame: A construction technique utilizing small-dimensioned lumber rather than large timbers.

Baluster: A small upright spindle or post, which, when used in a series, supports a handrail.

Balustrade: The entire railing system, which includes a handrail on top of a row of balusters and sometimes a bottom rail.

Bargeboard: A decorative board attached to the protruding edges of a gable roof. Often associated with Gothic Revival style. Also known as vergeboard.

Base: The part of a column below the shaft, or between the shaft and plinth or pavement. Also the wood, marble, or stone skirting at the bottom of a wall or room partition.

Batten: A strip of wood used for nailing across two or more other pieces.

Battlements: An indented, low wall that runs along the edge of the roof. Originated with Gothic designs of medieval England.

Bay Window: An alcove that projects from the outside wall with windows. May be round or multifaced.

Beak molding: A projecting molding with an out and downward curve on the exterior top, and a sharp break upward on the bottom of the projection; to form a drip, resembling a bird's beak.

Belvedere: A structure such as a cupola, designed to command a view.

Belt Course: A horizontal band around a building, usually with a molding.

Board and Batten: Vertical siding of wide boards, with strips laid vertically over the joints or grooves between the boards.

Bracket: A support for an overhanging balcony, cornice or shelf with an inverted "L" or triangular shape, in wood, stone or iron.

Buttress: A projecting pier from a wall, to create additional strength and take the thrust of an arch or the load of a beam.

Cable Molding: A torus or large bead molding with incised cuts imitating the twisting of a rope.

Cantilever: An unsupported beam or other member that projects beyond its supporting wall, sometimes under a cornice or eaves of a house.

Capital: The series of moldings or decoration above the shaft of a column or pilaster where the architrave rests.

Casing: Same as architrave; the trim around a door, window, or opening.

Castellated: Having battlemented parapet and turrets.

Cavetto: A concave or hollowed-out molding.

Center Ring: A plain, molded ring, or a floriated plaster cast ring decoration, for the center of the ceiling.

Chamfer: To cut away the exterior angle with a forty-five-degree bevel.

Channel: A groove or a series of grooves, elliptical in section, separated by arises or sharp edges, such as the channels in the shaft of the Doric Order.

Clustered Column: A number of engaged colonnettes grouped around a large column or a pier, close enough so that their bases and capitals combine as a single support.

Colonnade: A row of columns with their entablature; also a double row of columns.

Column: An upright member, circular in plan and usually slightly tapering. In classical architecture, it consists of a base, shaft, and capital. A column is designed to carry an entablature, or can be used ornamentally.

Conservatory: A small room, a bay projection, or a section of porch, with glazed exterior walls; a place to grow plants and flowers.

Coping: A stone, metal, terra cotta or other material placed on top of a wall or parapet to protect it from the weather.

Corbel: A bracket or projection from a wall, used to support a beam or arch.

Cornice: The upper division of the entablature: a molded projection that crowns or finishes the part to which it is affixed, as a wall, door, window, or pedestal.

Crenellated Parapet: A pattern of repeated alternate depressions; having battlements.

Cresting: A delicate, repeated ornament, incised, or resembling a small railing, carried along the top of a wall or roof.

Crocket: In Gothic architecture, a projecting block of stone or wood, carved, usually with foliage, to decorate a pinnacle on the inclined sides of spires and canopies.

Crown Molding: The molding at the top of the cornice.

Cupola: A small ornamental structure, square, round or octagonal; built on top of the roof; occasionally it is a small room.

Cusp: Terminal ending at the meeting points of the arcs in Gothic tracery.

Cyma: A molding whose section is a double curve, or wave-like in form.

Dentil: One of a band of small, square, tooth-like blocks that form a molding.

Dormer Window: A window in a sloping roof, usually in a sleeping room; derived from the French word "dormir," to sleep.

Double-hung Window: A window with a lower and upper sash that slide past each other.

Drip: A molding or projecting member with an edge that will drip the water and prevent it from running down the rest of the molding or the face of the building.

Eclectic Architecture: An architecture based on imitating any of the past styles, selecting a style by personal preference.

Encaustic: A method of painting decorations, using colors mixed in melted wax, which is kept hot during the process of painting.

Entablature: All that part of the horizontal construction above the columns. It is divided into three parts above the columns: architrave, frieze and cornice.

Eastlake: Exterior house decorations of a light, geometric style, as well as scroll and floral appliques on walls; named for furniture designer Charles Eastlake.

Eyebrow Window: A low, usually inward-opening window under the cornice in the architrave.

False Buttress: A buttress made of wood in a frame structure; a stone or brick buttress built in a wall, where none is structurally required; used merely as a design feature.

Fascia: A wide, flat, vertical member, used in combination with moldings, as the three horizontal bands into which the architraves of the Ionic and Corinthian entablatures are divided.

Festoon: A sculptured swag of leaves, flowers, or fruit suspended from two points.

Fillet: A narrow, flat, vertical band used for the separation of one molding from another; also the small, flat bands between the flutes of a column.

Finial: An ornament that crowns a pinnacle, spire or gable.

Fretwork: Ornamental openwork or intersecting bars in relief, usually minute and elaborate, in contrasting colors.

Frieze: The middle division of the entablature, between the cornice and the architrave.

Gable: The triangular portion of a wall, between the sloping lines of a pitched roof.

Greek Revival style: The Greek Revival style in England extended from about 1750 to 1850. In the United States, the style was at its height from 1820 to 1855.

Half-timbering: During the Gothic Revival style, in the timber frame construction, the open spaces were filled with brick or plaster, and the timber frame exposed. In the Eastlake period, the half-timber work was false, merely one-inch-thick boards, applied to the sheathing for embellishment.

Hipped Roof: A roof that slopes or pitches from all four sides.

Inglenook: A recess on one or both sides of a fireplace; it is usually provided with built-in seats.

Label Molding: A projecting molding over the top of an opening, and sometimes down a short distance on the sides of square openings. It is usually made with a concave cut and beveled edge to shed water.

Lancet Arch: A narrow, tall, sharply pointed window.

Lintel: A horizontal stone or piece of timber, spanning an opening in a wall, or resting across columns or piers.

Loggia: An arcaded or colonnaded passage, open on one or both sides.

Lunette: A semi-circular opening, either a window or a wall panel.

Mansard: A roof with a steep lower slope and flatter upper section, named after François Mansart; normally has four sides.

Modillion: An ornamental bracket under the soffit of the cornice.

Module: A unit of measurement from which all the parts of the order are proportioned. It is equal to one-half the diameter of the column at the base.

Mortise: A cavity cut into a piece of timber or other material, to accept a tenon.(see Tenon)

Motif: An element in a composition; a projecting central feature, or projecting ends framed with pilasters.

Mullion: The vertical dividing member between windows, windowpanes, or doors.

Muntin: The thin, wood or lead divisions in a window sash.

Neck: The part of a column between the astragal, at the end of the shaft, and the first molding of the capital.

Oculus: An element resembling an eye, especially a round window.

Order: Comprised of a column with base, shaft, and capital, plus an entablature that it supports. The Greeks used the Doric, Ionic, and Corinthian orders, to which the Romans added Tuscan and Composite.

Oriel: A curved or angular projecting window that is cantilevered out from the wall; similar to a bay window but often found on second stories.

Overmantel: Pilasters, paneling, shelving and mirrors, architecturally arranged in the space above the fireplace mantel.

Parapet: A low wall at the edge of a roof, balcony, terrace, battlement, etc.

Patera: A flat, round, or oval medallion, often used to ornament friezes.

Pavilion: The projecting part in the center of the facade, which is often especially embellished; also the projecting parts at the ends of a long facade.

Pediment: A low-pitched gable on top of the facade of a building, or a low triangular crown above a window or door; often associated with the Greek Revival style.

Pendant: A hanging ornament on roofs, ceilings, etc.; used primarily in Gothic architecture.

Peristyle: A series of columns, surrounding a temple or court.

Piazza: An open place surrounded by buildings; or a long, covered walk, with a roof supported by columns.

Pillar: A mass of stone, wood, or metal, standing upright on end and used as a support; the narrow masonry wall between windows, between a door and a window, or between doors.

Pierced Apron: A perforated panel of ornate design, placed in the apex of a gable; often associated with Gothic Revival style.

Pilaster: A flat, rectangular projection attached to a wall, with a capital, base or plinth block; used as a decorative representation of Classical columns.

Pinnacle: A small, turret-like projection on the top of a parapet, ridge, or buttress, often ornamented with crockets; primarily used in Gothic architecture.

Plinth: A plain block, square or rectangular in elevation, slightly larger than the base of the column or pilaster; used as a base.

Polychrome: Decorated in a variety of colors.

Porte-cochere: A roofed projection extending from the entrance over a driveway, through which vehicles can pass.

Portico: An entrance porch that has a roof supported by columns or brackets.

Quoins: Alternating blocks of stone or wood on a building corner, used to reinforce a wall and as a decorative element.

Roundel: A small circular window or panel; small bead molding.

Sash: Framework in which window lights are set.

Sawn Wood Ornament: Cut woodwork, used for trim on porches, eaves, fences, bargeboards, etc.; often called "gingerbread" scrollwork or fretwork.

Scoring: To divide a soft, plastered material with a metal tool, to imitate stone joints.

Shiplap Siding: Rebated, jointed boards to make a flush, weather-resisting, exterior wall siding.

Soffit: The under surface projection of the architrave between columns; the under surface of an arch.

Spandrel: The triangular space enclosed by the curve of an arch, the vertical of its springing, and the horizontal drawn from the level of its apex.

Spindle: Any slender, turned piece, as in a baluster. (see Baluster)

String Course: Continuous, horizontal band of stone, brick, or other building material, projecting beyond the building line or face of the wall.

Tenon: The end of a timber member cut to form a projection that fits into a mortise in another timber. (see Mortise)

Tracery: The ornamental detailing in the upper portion of a window.

Transom: Horizontal windows, usually with small lights over a door; a "transom" can also refer to the crossbars of windows.

Trefoil: A design similar to a cloverleaf; the centers of the leaves are the points of an equilateral triangle.

Tudor Arch: An elliptical arch drawn from three to five centers or a pointed arch drawn from four centers.

Tudor Flower: A cresting, carved from wood, with conventionalized leaves connected by a vine.

Vaulted Ceiling: An arched structure of masonry, forming a ceiling or roof.

Witch's Cap: A conical roof on a tower.

BIBLIOGRAPHY

AIDALA, Thomas & BRUCE, Curt
The Great Houses of San Francisco
Arch Cape Press, New York, NY 1987

ATHENAEUM OF PHILADELPHIA
Exterior Decoration
The Victorian Society in America, Philadelphia, PA 1976

BERG, Donald J.
Country Patterns
The Main Street Press, Pittstown, NJ 1986

BIRD, Roy
Topeka, An Illustrated History of the Kansas Capital

BRAMMER, Alex
Victorian Classics
Windgate Press, Sausalito, CA 1987

COLE, Tom
A Short History of San Francisco
Don't Call It Frisco Press, San Francisco, CA 1988

DELEHANTY, Randolph
Victorian Sampler
Foundation for San Francisco's Architectural Heritage,
San Francisco, CA 1979

DOWNING, Andrew Jackson
The Architecture of Country Houses
Dover Publications, New York, NY 1969

DOWNING, Andrew Jackson
Victorian Cottage Residences
Dover Publications, New York, NY 1981

FREEMAN, John Crosby
Victorian Entertaining
Running Press, Philadelphia, PA. 1989

GILLON, E. V. Jr. & LANCASTER, C.
Victorian Houses, A Treasury of Lesser Known Examples
Dover Publications, New York, NY 1973

GIROUARD, Mark
Sweetness and Light
Oxford University Press, Oxford, England 1977

HOLLY, Henry Hudson
Holly's Country Seats & Modern Dwellings
American Life Foundation, Watkins Glen, NY 1977

KEMP, Jim
Victorian Revival in Interior Design
Simon and Schuster, New York, NY 1985

KRAUS, Michael & DULLES, Foster Rhea
The United States, A Modern History
The University of Michigan Press, Ann Arbor, MI 1959

LEWIS, Arnold & MORGAN, Keith
American Victorian Architecture
Dover Publications, New York, NY 1975

MAAS, John
The Victorian Home in America
Hawthorn Books 1972

McALESTER, Virginia & Lee
A Field Guide To American Houses
Alfred A. Knopf, New York, NY 1984

MOSS, Roger
Century of Color
American Life Foundation, Watkins Glen, NY 1981

NAVERSEN, Kenneth
West Coast Victorians
Beautiful America Publishing Company, Wilsonville, OR 1987

NEVINS, Allan & COMMAGER, Henry S.
A Pocket History of the United States
Washington Square Press, New York, NY 1986

OLWELL, Carol & WALDHORN, Judith L.
A Gift to the Streets
St. Martin's Press, New York, NY 1976

PAUL, Tessa
The Art of Louis Comfort Tiffany
Exeter Books, New York, NY 1987

POMADA, Elizabeth & LARSEN, Michael
Daughters of Painted Ladies
E.P. Dutton, New York, NY 1987

POMADA, Elizabeth & LARSEN, Michael
The Painted Ladies Revisited
E.P. Dutton, New York, NY 1989

REECE, Daphne
Historic Houses of the Pacific Northwest
Chronicle Books, San Francisco, CA 1985

RIFKIND, Carol
A Field Guide to American Architecture
Plume, New York, NY 1980

ROTHMANN, Frances Bransten
The Haas Sisters of Franklin Street
Judah L. Magnes Memorial Museum, Berkeley, CA 1979

SAKACH, Tim & Deborah
American Historic Bed & Breakfast Inns
Association of American Historic Inns, Dana Point, CA 1987

SCHMIDT, Carl
The Victorian Era in the United States
New York, NY 1971

SCULLY, Vincent J. Jr.
The Shingle Style and The Stick Style
Yale University Press, New Haven, CT 1955

SIMPSON, Peter & HERMANSON, James
Port Townsend: Years That Are Gone
Quimper Press, Port Townsend, WA 1979

SINCLAIR, Peg & LEWIS, Taylor
Victorious Victorians
Holt, Rinehart & Winston, New York, NY 1985

SKJELVER, Mabel Cooper
Nineteenth-Century Homes of Marshall, Michigan
Marshall Historical Society, Marshall, MI 1971

STOVER, John F.
American Railroads
University of Chicago Press, Chicago, IL 1961

THE GEORGETOWN SOCIETY
Guide To The Georgetown Silver Plume
Cordillera Press, Inc., Colorado 1986

THOMAS, George E.
Cape May, An American Seaside Resort

WARREN, Scott & Beth
Victorian Bonanza
Northland Publishing, Flagstaff, AZ 1989

WELLMAN, Rita
Victoria Royal
American Life Foundation, Watkins Glen, NY 1970

WESPHAL, June
Eureka Springs

WILSON, Richard Guy
Victorian Resorts and Hotels
The Victorian Society In America, Philadelphia, PA 1982

WOODWARD, George E.
Woodward's Victorian Architecture and Rural Art
American Life Foundation, Watkins Glen, NY 1978

ACKNOWLEDGMENTS

We thank the following individuals for their valuable historical information and generous personal assistance during our travel, research, and production for *The Victorian Express*.

Beautiful America Publishing Company	Wilsonville, Oregon
Christine Bradley	County Archivist, Georgetown, Colorado
Bryce Holmes	Editor and Consultant, Seattle, Washington
Trish McDaniel and Olivia Meyer	Galveston Historical Society, Galveston, Texas
Alfie Mueller	Historian, Galena, Illinois
Robert Nugent	Tiffany Stained Glass, Chicago, Illinois
J. Robert Stewart	Lafayette Restoration Society, St. Louis, Missouri
Don and Mary Lou Vollmer	Denver, Colorado
Cecil Walker and June Wesphal	Eureka Springs Historical Museum, Eureka Springs, Arkansas
Laura Watt	Assistant Curator, Campbell House, St. Louis, Missouri
H. Scott Wolfe	History Center, Galena Public Library, Galena, Illinois
Joyce Woodard	Director Sales and Services, Topeka Convention and Visitors Bureau, Topeka, Kansas

We extend our gratitude to the following organizations for their involvement in the preservation of historical architecture in their communities. They encourage public awareness, education, and

Aspen Historical Society
620 West Bleeker Street
Aspen, Colorado 81611

Mid-Atlantic Center for the Arts
1048 Washington Street
Cape May, New Jersey 08204

Dubuque County Historical Society
P.O. Box 305
Dubuque, Iowa 52001

Eureka Springs Preservation Society
95 S. Main Street
Eureka Springs, Arkansas 72632

Galena State Historic Sites
908 Third Street
Galena, Illinois 61036

Galveston Historical Foundation
2016 Strand
Galveston, Texas 77550

Georgetown Society, Hamill House
Argentine Street
Georgetown, Colorado 80444

Marshall Historical Society
P.O. Box 68
Marshall, Michigan 49068

Lafayette Square Restoration Committee
2023 Lafayette Avenue
St. Louis, Missouri 63104

The Foundation For San Francisco's Architectural Heritage
2007 Franklin Street
San Francisco, CA 94109

Georgia Historical Society
Whitaker Street
Savannah, Georgia 31499

Topeka Convention & Visitors Bureau
120 E. Sixth Street
Topeka, Kansas 66603

ACKNOWLEDGMENTS

We especially appreciate the Victorian homeowners across America, whose dedication to restoring their residences provided us with a wealth of examples for *The Victorian Express*. To all the proud owners of Victorians, who have survived the financial challenges, endless repairs, and mixed blessings of architectural renovation, we offer the following consolation:

YOU KNOW YOU'VE GOT AN OLD HOUSE WHEN...

...a four-foot step ladder is useless to you.

...a six-foot Christmas tree is just too small.

...you'd rather read a paint-chip chart than the sports section.

...the living room light dims whenever you run the Dust Buster.

...the terms "warmth" and "patina" replace "worn out" and "dirty."

...the only man who knew where your city water shut-off is died in 1919.

...your change dish includes plaster washers, finish nails, and a radiator key.

...the local lumber yard can supply only one out of every ten items you want.

...you get more evening phone calls from siding salesmen than from your mother.

...you get personal Christmas cards from natural gas company executives you don't know.

...you start writing notes to future owners and hiding them behind the wainscoting and mop boards.

...everyone in town insists "that isn't the color the house used to be"-but no one remembers what color it was.

...you're willing to ruin your vision needlepointing upholstery for a footstool you could crush with one good squeeze.

...people are talking about "tennis elbow" or "Army aches" and you want to tell them about "scraper knuckle" and "rung foot."

...you walk four blocks in the dead of winter, refusing to park in the lot "they" built when they tore down the corner Victorian.

...when you're walking down that long upstairs hall, you feel as if someone is behind you, but you never, ever turn around to look.

...you think one of these days a loose attic floorboard will yield Old Man Smith's gold coins AND the original blueprints of the house.

INDEX

Aspen, CO, pp. 206-227
Benton, Thomas Hart, pp. 176, 182, 185
Black Hawk War, pp. 136, 153
Borden, Gail, p. 102
Button, Stephen D., pp. 43, 44, 45
Cape May, NJ, pp. 8, 10, 37-55,
Chicago, IL, pp. 106, 115, 117, 122, 143, 149, 198
Civil War, pp. 9, 16, 40, 65, 66, 72, 74, 79, 102, 106, 121, 141, 143, 147, 156, 162, 189, 192, 196, 198, 252
Clark, William, p. 174
Clayton, Nicholas J., pp. 100, 106, 107, 111
Compromise of 1850, p. 176
Cooke, Jay, pp. 44, 162
Crabtree, Lotta, p. 240
Crocker, Charles, pp. 251, 252
Crosswhite, Adam, p. 124
Davis, Andrew, p. 32
Downing, Andrew Jackson, pp. 10, 14, 32, 133, 134
Dubuque, IA, pp. 151-167
Eastlake, Charles, pp. 24, 26
Eastlake Style, pp. 24, 26, 32
Eureka Springs, AK, pp. 8, 77-93
Fenelon Place Elevator, p. 158
Financial Panic, pp. 8, 40, 156, 162-163, 176, 178, 192, 196, 207, 216
Fisk, James, pp. 147, 196
Folk Victorian Style, pp. 13, 30
Fowler, Orson S., pp. 18, 122
Fremont, John C., pp. 176, 230
Galena, IL, pp. 133-149
Galveston, TX, pp. 95-113
Georgetown, CO, pp. 207-227
Gothic Revival Style, pp. 13, 14, 16, 22, 24, 28, 32, 123, 151, 153, 156
Gould, Jay, pp. 147, 196
Grant, Ulysses S., pp. 20, 143, 147, 156, 164, 165
Graves, J. K., p. 158

Greek Revival, pp. 14, 32, 67, 114, 217
Holly, Henry Hudson, p. 32
Hopkins, Mark, pp. 251, 252
Huntington, Collis, pp. 251, 252
Italianate Style, pp. 13, 16, 22, 32, 50, 123, 151, 156, 217, 232
Jackson, Andrew, pp. 162, 176
Jackson, George, pp. 210, 212
Jefferson, Thomas, pp. 18, 152, 170
Kansas-Nebraska Act, p. 190
Leadville, CO, pp. 210, 216, 218, 222
Lewis, Meriwether, p. 174
Lincoln, Abraham, pp. 67, 72, 106, 145, 147
Louisiana Purchase, pp. 7, 134, 152, 172, 178
Manifest Destiny, pp. 7, 198, 230
Mansart François, pp. 10, 20
Marshall, MI, pp. 115-131
McKim, White, Emerson, Price, and Richardson, p. 24
Mexican War, pp. 147, 162
Mississippi River, pp. 7, 133-143, 151-153, 160, 164, 169, 170, 172, 173, 176, 178, 198
Missouri Compromise, pp. 178, 190
Mormons, pp. 154, 232
Napoleon, Louis, pp. 20, 170, 172
Nation, Carry A., p. 90
National Historic Landmark Districts, pp. 50, 87, 218, 226
New Orleans, LA, pp. 102, 153, 154, 169, 247
Octagon Style, pp. 13, 18, 122
O'Sullivan, John, p. 7
Pacific Railway Act, p. 198
Potwin Place, pp. 189-205
Potwin, Charles, pp. 189, 193, 194
Promontory, UT, pp. 198, 252
Pugin, A. W., p. 14
Queen Anne Style, pp. 13, 22-26, 30, 32, 64, 96, 110, 128, 151, 160, 170, 210, 217, 239, 253
Queen Victoria, pp. 7, 253

Railroad, Atchison, Topeka & Santa Fe, pp. 191, 192, 196-199
Railroad, Central of Georgia, p. 62
Railroad, Central Pacific, pp. 198, 252
Railroad, Chicago, Burlington & Northern, p. 160
Railroad, Eureka Springs, p. 80, 82
Railroad, Frisco Line, p. 80
Railroad, Illinois Central, p. 138
Railroad, Michigan Central, pp. 120, 121, 123
Railroad, Northern Pacific, p. 198
Railroad, Santa Fe, pp. 189, 192, 197, 203
Railroad, Southern Pacific, pp. 192, 196
Railroad, Union Pacific, pp. 192, 196, 198, 199, 252
Revolutionary War, pp. 58, 60, 62, 67, 170
Richardson, Henry Hobson, pp. 10, 28, 56
Romanesque Revival Style, pp. 13, 28, 69, 110
San Francisco, CA, pp. 8, 10, 32, 229-255
Savannah, GA, pp. 57-75
Second Empire Style, pp. 13, 20-22, 32, 38, 151, 156, 175, 182, 217
Shaw, Richard Norman, pp. 10, 22, 28
Sherman Silver Act, pp. 163, 216
Sherman, William, pp. 67, 72,
Shingle Style, pp. 24, 32
Showboats, p. 140
Spanish-American War, p. 7
St. Louis, MO, pp. 7, 106, 138, 147, 152, 153, 169-187, 198
Stanford, Leland, pp. 251, 252
Stick Style, pp. 24, 32, 151, 193,
Sutter, John A., p. 233, 235
Tiffany, Louis Comfort, pp. 34, 92, 156
Topeka, KS, pp. 189-205
Twain, Mark, p. 173, 247, 250
Whitney, Eli, p. 60

ABOUT THE AUTHORS

Kristin Holmes

Kristin Holmes, the architectural historian, researcher, and co-author of *The Victorian Express*, owns an interior design business on the island of Maui. She studied interior design at the Artisan School of Design in Honolulu. Kristin is a member of The Victorian Society in America and the National Trust for Historic Preservation. This book represents Kristin's lifelong desire to share her passionate view of the Victorian legacy.

David Watersun

David Watersun is a photographer and writer based in Hawaii. His work is commissioned internationally by advertising, corporate, and editorial clients for books, magazines, and publications. He holds degrees in Communications from Occidental College in Los Angeles and Commercial Photography from Brooks Institute in Santa Barbara. David specializes in location assignments that feature architecture, travel, and culture.

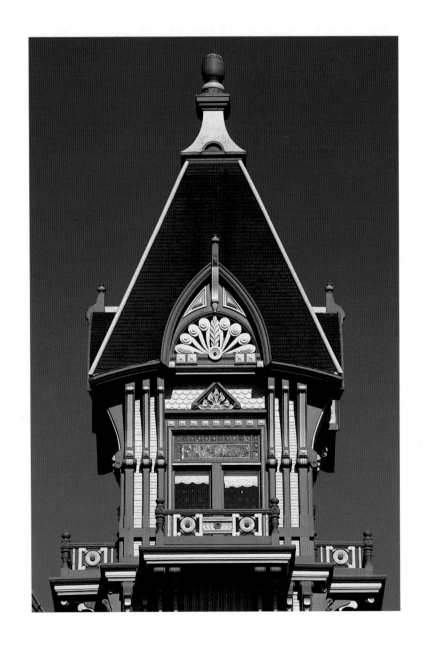